Social Media Marketing:

The Jargon-Free Guide to Simple Social Media Marketing Success

LEWIS LOVE

ISBN: 1499555377
ISBN-13: 978-1499555370

CONTENTS

ACKNOWLEDGMENTS

I would like to thank every single person who has purchased or downloaded any of my previous books. Without your encouraging feedback, this book would not have been possible. I would also like to thank every single person I have worked with over the past three years. Without whom I would not have the holistic knowledge that has helped to create so many of your online presences.

1 INTRODUCTION

I've previously written two books on social media marketing: "Facebook Business Basics" and "Twitter Business Basics". Each addressed the two biggest social networks respectively. They have helped thousands of small business owners and entrepreneurs take their business into the social realm.

The last few years has seen an explosion in the amount of content shared through social services such as Facebook, Twitter and Google+. Although search engines treat socially shared links differently than other types of links, they notice them nonetheless. There is much debate among search professionals as to how exactly search engines factor social link signals into their algorithm, but there is no denying the rising importance of social channels. The last three years has seen social media move from an uncertain strategy to an undeniable force behind the success of start-ups and established businesses alike. Every marketer now has their finger on the pulse of social media, keeping up-to-date with the latest offerings from Facebook, Twitter and Google+. No one has benefited more than small business owners and start-ups though. Social media plays a pivotal role in these businesses and this book will look at why that is.

It's important to point out at this early stage that marketing is not purely about boosting your sales. Sure, increase in revenues is always nice, but marketing encompasses many more parts of your business than you possibly realise. Marketing, especially on social platforms, affects your customer services, product development, merchandising and retail arms. You need to keep this in mind when reading this book and implementing advice, both techniques draw directly from here and from other resources.

My TED Talk

TED (Technology, Entertainment and Design) talks are a set of conferences that take place all over the world. Run by a non-profit organisation, Sapling-Foundation, the conferences aim to disseminate 'ideas worth spreading'. What this often leads to is emotionally charged speeches by some of the best speakers in the world, offering their ideas as the righteous path. This section will possibly sound like one of those TED talks. I make no apologies for this. Unfortunately, it has to be included, as too many people still believe in quick fixes and overnight success. Fuelled by the brainwashing power of moronic business coaches, offering '4 Steps to Quick Success' and 'Double your revenue with this one piece of advice', many entrepreneurs have succumbed to the idea that business is about growing quickly, becoming a millionaire and living off the fortunes you create. In reality, this seldom happens. Generally business is a slow, and sometimes painful process of growth and decline. The mark of a great entrepreneur or business owner is one that can foresee the decline, or at least prepare for it, and then recover effectively. Decline, I would argue is a good thing. It shows sustainability. Constant growth cannot continue forever; get used to it.

Business shouldn't be about the bottom-line. It should be about making the world a better place. If you can't look at yourself in the morning and say, 'my products, services or advice enrich or enhance the lives of others', I would question your motives. If you sell cars, are they roadworthy machines or just scraps of metal designed to get off the forecourt but not much further? If you offer advice on travel destinations, do you recommend places that you know the customer will love, or do you just opt for the easiest sell with the highest commission? Think about it for a minute, because if you were just going for those high-profit margins, without a care for the consumer, I would recommend you stop reading here. This book offers advice on how to enhance your social media, by giving, not receiving. Giving back to your consumers, providing free advice, sending birthday wishes without expecting to generate a sale as a result. It isn't about trying to directly drive your sales, although as you will see, this is a convenient by-product of your philanthropic, social efforts.

I've worked with some really talented people, leaders in

their respective fields, and they've all had a hunger to create the best possible products. These guys (and girls), needless to say, are all very successful at what they do. I've also been lucky enough to work with some people who are just passionate about the business they are in, not for making a profit, but for making their customers happy. A lot of people are like this. They care about their business, but aren't that interested in the product itself, especially when it comes to using it. Think of a stationary salesman; does he really have a passion for paper? You don't need to be that passionate about the products directly though; it's about being passionate about your audience and consumers. The paper salesman cares about his customers, so he sources the best quality paper for the fairest price, offering the greatest possible service. Paradoxically, he does care about his product, but that is only because he cares about his customers, who in turn, do care about the product.

A little while back, I had the opportunity of working with two great women, each of whom sold fine jewellery. For the purpose of anonymity, we'll call them Thelma and Louise, although I would like to point out that neither of them have made a hobby of homicide. Well, not to my knowledge. Thelma imported her jewellery, selling them on her website and at specific events. Louise on the other hand, made all the jewellery herself. Obviously Louise's jewellery costs a tad more, but she also sold them through similar channels. They were both equally successful at what they did, targeting slightly different markets. What surprised me however, and opened my eyes to the world of 'doing good in business', was they both cared tremendously about their customers. I was expecting

Louise to be somehow more 'in touch' with her customers and products, after all she made them (the product that is). I thought Thelma would only be interested in the profit margins - that is why you import isn't it? Well it turns out importing is a lot harder than it sounds. Thelma had to travel to India to source the stones, picking them each out individually. These then had to be drilled, cast or whatever other magic was performed before being imported into the UK. I was pleasantly surprised, and it made me realise, Thelma and Louise were both in the business of 'doing good'.

So how does this relate to social media and, in particular, Facebook? Well, we should care. We should care about our products and we should care about our customers. We should be 'doing good' in everything we do, and when it comes to social media, it's even more vital!

This book doesn't have the answer to getting a million, or even a thousand Facebook 'Likes'. Instead, it's got some sound advice about harnessing the Likes you do have and making the most of your current fans. Think about this for a second; how much is a Facebook Like worth to you? Well if you've been working hard already, you may know how much traffic Facebook brings your site or business, the conversion rate of the traffic and a rough idea about how much each Like is worth. Great! If I give you a sneaky way to get a thousand more Likes though, do you honestly believe that conversion rate will continue? Of course it won't. As your engagement with the users drops, so does the conversion rate. What I'd much rather see businesses doing, is enhancing their conversion rates from their current social traffic; that way when new fans come along you're already set up to better help them, and as such, convert them. We shouldn't be preparing our Facebook pages and Twitter feeds for constant growth. Keep in mind that a bit of decline is probably just around the corner. This helps us to remember to look after the early-adopters, instead of just chasing after the new Likes. Social media, and business in general is a funny kettle of fish. I've waffled on about 'doing good in business', but then I also mention conversion rates and customers. It's easy to lose sight of it all. In reality, businesses need to make a profit, or at least self-sustain. With this in mind, conversion rates and customers are required; without them, we can't 'do good' at all. But if we remember, and make it our sole goal to 'do good', I'd suggest we could all make our own worlds a slightly more enjoyable place.

My Style of Business and Who It Helps

I don't believe in "one size fits all" at the best of times but especially when it comes to business. I feel that business advice has to be tailored to the business and as such no one person or consultant can be an expert for every business. Or at least, they can't be the right expert.

I don't claim to be the best social media consultant for every business. In fact, I don't claim to be the best – full stop. I believe there's always more to learn and that's what makes, for me, the online world and social media so exciting. This being said, I do understand where my experience and expertise lies.

The businesses that I help the most and those who get the most out of my advice are those who occupy somewhat of a middle ground in their market. I don't work particularly well with businesses that compete on price.

That's because one of my firm beliefs is that if you compete on price and someone comes and undercuts you you've got nowhere to go. It's a race to the bottom, and that is all you have got to compete with. Price. Poundland worked well, until the 99ps Stores came along.

On the other hand I don't always work too well with high end, luxury brands. It's a market that is difficult to define and as soon as you begin to market and educate the market surrounding the higher end products you by default actually lessen the luxurious nature of the products. Ironically, I have written and published articles about the paradoxical nature of luxury brands, and whilst that work was well received, it hasn't made me any better working within that environment.

Whilst there are experts out there that can offer advice for these two ends of the market it's not where I sit. Where I sit is in the middle. The businesses that compete on service rather than price. Those that offer excellent products at a fair price. They might have some more luxurious offerings yet they don't distinguish themselves as luxury brands.

When it comes to social media I think it's important to remember this. If you run a luxury brand you might struggle with the advice in this book, or any of my books. The same can be said for brands who occupy the lower end of the market. That's not to say that I don't agree with those ends of the market. I'm more than happy to purchase products from a budget retailer to save a few pounds here and there. And I'm also more than happy to "splash the cash" at the right moment and opt for a more high end product. But when it comes to offering advice, my expertise lies in the mid-market.

If you are a business owner whose business occupies either the lower or the higher end of the market, don't be put off by this though. There will still be some truths that run through social media marketing which will apply to every end of the market.

Things like staying social and being consistent are things that are important no matter where you place your brand.

A Note on Social Media Managers

Whilst social media consultants can be worth their weight in gold, for small businesses and large corporations alike, I feel it can be a waste of money and ability to ask these experts to help with basic social media marketing setup, techniques and troubleshooting. That is why I have written this book; to serve as a handbook to those who feel they need a helping hand or a bit of advice starting out, and to also save them money that would have been spent on the experts. This book looks at the basics of Facebook for businesses, offering itself as an introduction into a rapidly evolving field. It is aimed at those who are bewildered by the social-sphere and need some friendly guidance in taking the first tentative steps into a world of Likes and viral campaigns. It may also benefit those who have dived into Facebook without assessing the situation first, serving as a rescue guide.

Social media managers can be a Godsend to businesses, especially for those that really have no idea what they're doing on social media. Social media managers should be experienced in all things social media, and they will be able to help you get on the right networks and create the best strategies to engage your audience and generate interest in your brand.

There are certain qualities that this individual needs to possess however. A social media manager needs to get into everyone's business. In order to know how to promote your company, they need to know what everyone in your office is working on and what their responsibilities are. An outgoing individual will have no problem reaching out to all of your employees and trying to learn more about what makes your office tick. Plus, outgoing people will be able to reach out and connect more with your social audience, which is the ultimate point.

Market places such as Elance and oDesk have sprung up over recent years and whilst they are great for certain jobs (I even use them myself for transcribing audio for example), they can be dangerous to use for hiring social media managers.

That's not to say there aren't great social media marketers on these market places, it's just there are a lot of people who profess to be proficient in social media marketing where in fact they don't know enough.

Social media is not something that can be managed whenever - it needs to be managed constantly. Your social media manager needs to be hard working, so that they can spend their time: researching the best social platforms for your business, creating accounts, creating an image for your brand on these accounts, and communicating with your audience. They need to answer questions and comments immediately, and they need to have regular posts in order to engage your audience.

Most of your social media postings are going to involve text, so it's very important that your social media manager knows how to write. If they can't string a sentence together, or if they misspell every other word, it's going to reflect poorly on your brand. Your social media manager also has to know what tone to use. Does your company want to come off as strictly informative, or do you want to be witty and humorous? It's very important that this is decided upon early on, and that your social media manager can convey the tone. If your company starts to mix up tones, it's going to be extremely confusing to your social following.

Social media is more than just Facebook, and it's very important that your social media manager knows this. A successful social media manager will have the knowledge and expertise needed to run a campaign on any network, and they can use this knowledge to help your business determine which platforms are the best options for your goals. Your social media manager also needs to know the line between public info and confidential info. Your business may have some information that should not be public knowledge, and it's very important that your social media manager does not share anything confidential with your fans and followers.

A social media manager can greatly improve the success of your company's social media campaigns. If you want to hire a great social media manager, make sure they possess the above qualities. I would suggest however, that this book should be able to bring you up to speed with all things social (especially Facebook), and of course as you immerse yourself with the social network, you'll pick up all sorts of knowledge along the way. This knowledge will be beneficial to you, whether or not you decide to outsource your social media management to a professional at a later date.

The reason it's so important to get your social media manager right, is that they are taking control of your brand within a social field. You wouldn't outsource your customer relations in real life to somebody who didn't know about or didn't care about your business. It's a job that you need to take great time and care over choosing the right applicant. They need to be able to spell correctly every time and convey the tone of your brand correctly.

If you're a traditional British company with strong British values and you employ an Australian social media marketer, you could find your brand weakening within social media.

Likewise, if you're an Australian brand, I might not be the best person to manage it for you. You'll notice how sometimes though you do need someone to manage your social media. I'm certainly not saying it's a bad thing. After all, I earn a living from managing other people's social media accounts. It's my profession.

I do however regularly turn down clients. Partly because I'm usually always fully booked and I try not to work with more than four clients at a time. That is partly because there is only so many hours in a day, but also because when I'm working with more than four brands, I begin to lose the tone or worse, the tones start to merge together with each brand.

I've also learnt in recent years that you can't manage a social media campaign for a brand in any less than 15 hours a week. 3 Hours a day, Monday to Friday gives me enough time to get my mind in place for the brand, come up with some engaging content and reply to the comments and messages that have been sent as we'll find out later in the book.

Engaging with your fans on social media networks, whether that's Google+, Facebook, Twitter or LinkedIn, is vital. If you don't engage, you won't succeed. All you will be doing is shouting a message that no one will want to hear.

So social media managers could be excellent for you. They can free up your time, which is invaluable if you're a small business or a startup with limited hours and limited resources. However, they don't come cheaply and you can't expect someone to manage your brand efficiently on social media in just a couple of hours a week.

It takes a lot of time, hard work and dedication to make social media work so you should expect to pay accordingly.

Social media managers can be great for your brand but they can also be very damaging.

Remember: Picking the wrong social media manager can have a negative effect on your brand and business.

Also remember that social media marketing can work two ways. If you get it right, the sales can increase almost exponentially depending on your business type. But if you get it wrong, you could see sales drop if the person you bring in to manage your brand on social media doesn't know what they're doing, can't spell correctly and sends out messages which are inappropriate for your target audience, or just plain boring.

You could see your loyal customers leaving you for your competitors. It's not something you should stay up at night worrying about, it's just some food for thought. Choose your social media manager wisely.

Outsourcing Your Social Media Management

In today's volatile markets and advancing technology, marketing is becoming ever more complicated, imposing the need for outsourcing some services like social media marketing. While some businesses have succeeded in managing their own social media campaigns, using Twitter as a marketing tool can be difficult to deal with because the social network can be unpredictable.

One of the factors that may make you feel that outsourcing is the right way to go is when your business has been managing its own social media campaign, and then realised that it does not have the man power, or expertise to cope. The main reason this happens though, is when there is lack of concentration. A committed employee is the one who has minimal duties. If a business is unwilling or unable to dedicate the required number of workers to man the social media accounts, their campaign may not produce good results and they will often opt to outsource.

In any business venture, there must be proper supervision and co-ordination. People need to know what they are doing too. Tweeting about your personal life is very different to Tweeting for business. When a business adopts social media as a marketing tool, it must set up a managing person or panel. But in most cases, there is a tendency to economise by using the existing management. This normally fails because the managers may not have knowledge or experience in the new world of social media. When outsourcing, management expenses are normally lower because supervisors and managers of outsourcing firms can monitor the operations for many businesses.

Social media agencies have the experience in their job. Better still, they have pre-established ways of conducting their business. This gives them the edge in terms of results. A company that is being defeated because their business rivals have their social media campaigns managed and run by experts will find it difficult to resist the services of an agency.

One of the challenges in business is dealing with market dynamics. Usually, companies keep on changing their operations. Dictated by market forces, changing consumer tastes and advancing technology, they continually adopt new products and drop those which are no longer in demand. How many times have you gone to the supermarket to pick up your favourite snack, only to discover they've changed the recipe, or worse, taken the item off the shelf entirely! Then there comes the issue of products whose demand peaks during certain seasons. With all this stuff to take care of, balancing the marketing is complicated, particularly for small or medium enterprises. They therefore often choose to outsource some or all marketing matters.

Fighting a losing battle is not appealing to anyone. Rather than see whether they can succeed and run the risk of failure, some business owners opt for outsourcing their social media marketing from the get-go. Some agencies can demonstrate in a credible manner the certainty of achievement. Others though, offer less certain promises. I can't tell whether certain companies are worth their weight or not, I can't even tell you that outsourcing is the right thing to do. I make a living off creating and running other peoples' internet marketing and social media campaigns, so it would be foolish of me to say that it is a bad thing to do. Instead, I'll offer as balanced a view as I can, allowing you to make the decision confidently.

Benefits of Outsourcing Social Media Management

In the modern world, internet marketing is now shifting gears to focus on social media as it becomes a popular and effective channel. But without the appropriate tools, social media marketing can become a headache. That is why businesses, particularly small and medium ones, are outsourcing.

One of the advantages of outsourcing social media is that the sharing sites need constant monitoring. For example, businesses which have established themselves properly on Twitter may find that they receive millions of tweets in a short time. All of these will need a response from the business. If this is not forthcoming, the trend may change for the worst, with followers turning away from the company.

Outsourcing agents will usually not only promise a good outcome, they will also have the framework for gauging and demonstrating that their strategies actually work. In some cases, such agents will also offer a free trial for a limited period of a few days. In doing so, they give the client the confidence that they will surely deliver and the client will have the comfort of watching what can be achieved. If results can be apparent in a few days, however small, this can be reason enough to continue the relationship. Of course, you'll have to remember to define what the goals are, and remember that follower count *does not count*.

In any business adventure, the cost versus benefit analysis is a vital tool in evaluating any undertaking. When a company's own employees have the responsibility of responding to issues on social media, it may be difficult to ascertain the portion of such workers salary as expenditure against this marketing strategy. Secondly, there is a high likelihood of these employees being overworked, or they just don't have the expertise. Just because an employee spends their free time on Twitter, it doesn't necessarily mean they are cut out to handle the corporate account. With outsourcing, you are constantly aware of what costs to cover.

Companies who have specialised in offering services on the behalf of other businesses are bound to be vigilant in their work. This is because they are dedicated to this service. It follows that they will do everything in their power to do their best in building their reputation and hence attract more companies to their services. Moreover, they stand in a better position of monitoring how the social climate is fairing. I'm constantly reading about the latest happenings; this research time is factored into my clients fees, but ultimately, this is what keeps me ahead of the pack and allows me to offer a superior service to what they could manage in-house. I will, for example, monitor the most sought-after keywords, choose the relevant content to tweet about, and use it to work with clients to perfect their work.

When a business decides to carry out the work of social media marketing, there is a risk that their work may not produce any tangible results. This risk is aggravated by the fact that the business owners will usually not have in place the appropriate apparatus for monitoring their progress. In such a case, it may be too late for the business to start all over again and try to catch up. Much time will already be wasted and all the funds invested will essentially be money down the drain.[1] While they are at it, their competitors could already have the lion's share.

Although nothing is set in stone, sometimes letting experts do the work for you keeps you on the safer side of things. Social media management companies will give you advice to ensure that you encompass all fundamentals into your campaign. This will give you the peace of mind of knowing that your business is in good hands.

Working without a budget is like planting your own time bomb. Although not all budgets are fixed, working on a budget is a very effective managerial tool. When a firm is outsourcing for certain services, a pre-determined budget becomes a reality. The outsourcing company can discuss the details of a tailor-made budget with the client. Such an arrangement will make it possible to examine the contribution the venture will have created, over and above the normal projections.

All marketing tactics are aimed at producing good results, but defining what good results are may not be simple. Coupled with the fact that you may be working on a certain campaign, believing it to be working, but with absolutely no evidence pointing towards your goals and all of a sudden, the idea of social media management becomes more enticing. Any reputable marketing agency will warn businesses of any looming danger and should instruct them, or even help them to employ the necessary defense mechanisms. As you can see, outsourcing your social media can have many benefits for small businesses.

---

[1] Or 'put down to experience'.

Negative Aspects of Social Media Management

I've spent a long time detailing the benefits of outsourcing your social media management. Of course, I would say that; I make a large part of my living from managing other business's social profiles. What I'll outline now though, is why it isn't always best to outsource. I'm not one to make a quick buck. If I can see a business won't see any benefit from me looking after their social accounts, or worse, I'll end up crippling their finances, I will be honest with them. Unfortunately, it seems much of the world isn't like me, with many consultants out to make money without a care for the client. That's why I've included this section. Hopefully you'll be able to see why outsourcing your social media can be risky at times.

Finding an agency or consultant who will care for your business like your own is difficult. It's obvious that no one can understand your business like you do. Your mode of service to your customers cannot compare to that of other parties. This is because you identify better with your customers. In so doing, you get to know them that little bit better. For some, outsourcing your social media is like outsourcing your customer relations. Would you employ somebody with no track record, or someone you've never met to welcome customers to your store? What about the waiters at your new restaurant; would you hire somebody who didn't care about the food you served? Probably not. But you would hire somebody that was passionate about your business or products. It's a tricky one, especially when agencies and consultants exaggerate what they can achieve to entice potential clients. Of course, the picture on the can does not necessarily correspond with the contents. If you happen to make a hasty decision and fall into the hands of an unscrupulous agency, the consequences can be devastating. In order to select the most suitable outsourcing firm, you must do enough research. You must look at the track record of those offering such services and be acquainted with what they have accomplished for their other customers. If they do not have any appealing results, chances are that they will not deliver.

Another pitfall in outsourcing social media management is that the agency might not be able to keep track of the dynamics of your trade. These agents are well updated with the changing trends in the social media platform, but they may not automatically adapt with the changing business climate. Without proper communication with them, they may continue targeting an audience that is already out of the market. Worse still, they may answer questions regarding products which, unbeknown to them, you no longer produce or sell. Secondly, they may lack responses about new products. This can greatly confuse rather than help potential customers.

Some outsourcing agencies will do a very good job in launching your campaign in the social media. This is what they are good at. However, some won't offer any additional services, such as ongoing management. Should this be the case, the campaign may not have any long-term benefits. For a client to seek such services, they must be confident that they will be able to carry on the rest. Proper supervision and training may be offered, and is an ideal way to prevent the problems which can arise when you realise that you do not have the know-how to manage the campaign.

As a client, you are on the safer side if you understand the agency or consultant you are hiring, and the contract. In some cases, you could have the misunderstanding that your job ends after the negotiations with the outsourcing firm are over. In reality, this isn't always the case and you should understand what your responsibilities and duties are before signing the contract. If such a detail is ignored, the work of the agency can become harder and harder. It is best for the client to appreciate the fact that although the agency is being paid to carry out the work, they will continually require more information, and sometimes a helping hand. Some agreements I have with clients allow me to take the lead on everything. As far as efficiency is concerned, this is great, both for me and the client. I take care of everything, from campaign planning, to blog writing. It allows me to get a lot done, quickly. But for others, and this isn't necessarily a bad thing, they like to hold on to a bit more control. They want to discuss my ideas through, often requesting three alternatives when it comes to campaign planning. If this is the route you choose to take with your social media management, you'll need to be aware that by outsourcing, you may not actually save yourself any time, as you'll be on the phone and emailing the agency or consultant fairly regularly.

When considering outsourcing, in-depth knowledge of the agency or consultant is vital. I'm not talking about where they live or what colour socks they choose to wear, but you should be asking yourself a few questions. How much do you know about them? Can you actually trust them to do stuff on your behalf? What other businesses are they working for? If among their clients is your competitor, they are bound to be biased and will not deliver the best results. For an agency to work properly for you, they must uphold strict discretion where necessary. If certain information is leaked to your competitors, they may use it against you. Additionally, you must also be certain that the agent is of high standing and will not engage in any shoddy deals. Whilst 'black-hat' marketing techniques and dodgy schemes are generally reserved for SEO (search engine optimisation), there is an increasing trend for some shady agency to opt for these 'quick-fixes', such as buying followers, something I have already explained is a terrible thing to do.

For you to consider whether to outsource or to do it yourself, you've got to ask yourself many questions. Do you have the tools and experience to do the work yourself? How much do you understand about the social media platform? There is no clear-cut solution towards making a good decision. The solution is based on how you answer the questions. Some businesses may find it helpful to find an agency for launching a social media campaign and later hiring permanent employees specifically to manage and update. If you opt to outsource, you must obtain an agency or consultant that will grasp the mission and vision of your business, be enthusiastic about your products and have a clear-cut idea of what they can achieve, including the time frame. They must also value your target market as well as being in constant communication with you.

Is Social Media Important?

No matter how hard you try to avoid engaging with the Internet, it is becoming a more and more impossible endeavor. It is through the worldwide web that people from different continents are becoming connected, how loved ones are staying up to date, how businesses are doing business. Almost all human transactions can be found online, be it relationships or purchasing, making the world more accessible and reachable than it was. So if you wish to have some power and influence amongst the crowd, you need to embrace the Internet and social media.

When it comes to business, it is very important to stand out and stay ahead of the competition. One sure-fire way to do this is by making an online presence and keeping it active. Businesses now need an online presence if they wish to really succeed, and starting out with the most powerful site on the Internet is a good place to start. Why? Because not only does it allow people to connect or network with each other, but now it also has special features for businesses to utilise, that they may market, promote, and advertise their services or products to the billions of users registered on the network.

Social Media Marketing cannot be understated. Its roll in online business is increasing year on year and my prediction is that this will continue to rise in the forthcoming years. While search engine optimization has been on the lips of every marketer for the past ten years, I feel the next ten years will be the years of social.

Having a Facebook page has become an essential marketing tool for some businesses; it allows them to interact with their current and potential customers while also providing information and being entertaining. However, equally as many new businesses don't see the benefit of having a social presence. Some businesses feel that Facebook, Twitter or Google+ may not be right for them, but as potential customers lead an increasingly online life, the importance of having a presence on these sites grows too.

The thing to remember is, just because you have an account for every single social network out there, it doesn't mean that you will have more sales at the end of the month. It takes connection, an established relationship and consistency to be able to gain results. You also need to connect to the right kind of people, otherwise your efforts will drive awareness but not sales.

You also need to constantly inform your audience with timely and relevant news about your products and services. If you can, try to share information about other things that are not about you but still relate to your brand and products. You need to give them valuable information so that they can see you as someone of value.

Be wary of having to please too many friends and followers. They don't necessarily translate to buying customers. If you take a good look at it, what percentage of these people actually buys from you?

Even with this in mind, most marketers find that social media, and Facebook in particular, help them to create and market stand-out businesses in noisy marketplaces. Small business owners however, have many things to juggle in their time. One day they will be head of marketing, another day they'll be the chief financial officer - so trying to allow time for social media isn't always high on the priority list. Research has shown though, that building social media accounts is a great way to build long-lasting connections and brand loyalty. It probably won't turn your start-up into an overnight success, but it will help secure repeat business and steady growth for years to come.

The power of endurance is apparent when you talk to those who have been actively engaging in social media on a regular basis for three or more years. It's by no means a medium where you can see quick results, and for this reason, the social networking scene isn't for everyone. The important decision to make is whether or not you can invest the required amount of time, over an extended period. Too many marketers decide that Facebook is the way forward, give it a go, even doing it correctly, for six months, but then give up because they're not seeing the return on investment they were hoping for. Of course you do need to set a cut-off point - investing hours every week for five years with absolutely no return or sales to show for it isn't what you want, so set some targets and reassess as you hit or miss them.

Which Channel is Right for You?

Whilst there is certainly a school of thought that suggests you should be everywhere, and I tend to agree that that's the right move to make if possible, it's also important to state at this early stage that if you're already on Facebook, Twitter, Pinterest or LinkedIn, you've got a strategy and it's already taking up too much time, adding another social network into the frame is not a good move. Some businesses work better on certain social networks. Cupcake businesses for example, work very well on Pinterest, but you might find a business advisor is more suited to LinkedIn. These are generalisations though and there's no reason why a business advisor couldn't rock it on Pinterest and a cupcake maker couldn't be awesome on LinkedIn. It's all about finding out what works for you and what works for your business. There really is no right or wrong answer. The only right thing to do is to make sure whatever you do, you do well. If that means only taking up the reins on one social network at a time, that's fine. Don't over stretch yourself because all you'll do is diminish any effect that your efforts will have.

If you're a one-man-band, like many small businesses are, or if you're just starting out, remember that you don't have to be on every social network. Pick one, maybe two and do it well. With that being said, if you do have more resources (money or time), being on more than one social network is a massive advantage. Why? Well, different social networks attract different groups of people.

Twitter has a relatively young crowd whereas Pinterest is made up by predominately female users. What this means is your business can reach different groups of people. Whilst this might not apply to every business I do feel that the more people you can reach the higher your chances of success with social media marketing.

I worked with a plumber who had a good presence on Facebook but was unsure about whether any other networks were applicable to him. After only a short period, he was rocking it on Twitter as well. But then he came back to me and asked whether there'd be any point going for Pinterest.

After sitting down and sorting out strategy we realized there was a missive gap in the market. Whilst the users are predominately female, and the pins generally tend to revolve around cupcakes, nice interiors and cute cats, with a few clever images (some of which were rather tenuously linked) he really enhanced his presence online and reached a whole new group of people: female users aged between

20 and 35.

Female users aged between 20 and 35 still need a plumber every now and again and who would they go to? The Yellow pages? AAA Plumbing? Or to the plumber that they've built up a relationship with on Pinterest already? They go back to him.

This is one example of how businesses that you may have thought to be irrelevant to certain social networks can in fact work very well. If none of your competitors are using it that might be a sign that it's not worth doing, however I like to think of it as an open opportunity. If none of your competitors are using it – that market's yours. Go out and grab them and make the most of them.

2 FACEBOOK

The last three years has seen social media move from an uncertain strategy to an undeniable force behind the success of start-ups and established businesses alike. Every marketer now has their finger of the pulse of social media, keeping up-to-date with the latest offerings from Facebook, Twitter and Google+.

No one has benefited more than small business owners and start-ups though. Social media marketing plays a pivotal role in these businesses and this book will look at why that is and how you can build on these successes.

This section will benefit those who have dived into Facebook without assessing the situation first, serving as a rescue guide. It is also aimed at those who are bewildered by the social-sphere and need some friendly guidance in taking the first tentative steps into a world of 'Likes' and 'viral campaigns'.

A Brief History of the Biggest Social Media Platform

Facebook arguably started when Mark Zuckerberg decided to create a college platform. Of course, he probably never thought it would become the overnight success it did. While attending college as an undergraduate at Harvard University, Zuckerberg experimented on a program which potholed campus students together for members to decide who was more attractive. The website was known as Facemash, which was later shutdown by the school administration for 'security issues'.

As a social networking site, Facebook has revolutionised the way in which people chat to friends and family, but it didn't start out like that. Notwithstanding the inconvenient incident surrounding Facemash, Zuckerberg began writing new code in January 2004 for a new website known as TheFacebook. Joined by his other colleagues in his own college dorm room, Zuckerberg wanted the site to help Harvard College students connect with each other. As computer programmers, Zuckerberg along with his four college colleagues; Eduardo Saverin, Andrew McCollum, Dustin Moskovitz, and Chris Hughes began using their skills to help students at Harvard create a closer tie. Their main aim was to create a web service that would help people share information by viewing profiles of those that are part of their network. The combined talent of these five men resulted in the creation of Facebook, which was first used by Harvard University as an online system for student monitoring and a steadfast management of online college-related tasks. TheFacebook, which was originally located at thefacebook.com, was launched on February 4,

2004. In the first few days of its creation, TheFacebook was bombarded with controversies as to who the real founder was. Three Harvard students, Cameron Winklevoss, Tyler Winklevoss, and Divya Narendra accused Zuckerberg of stealing the idea from them, leading them to create another website known as HarvardConnect. However, the accusation did not prosper and the case was settled leaving TheFacebook alive and thriving. Its membership was initially limited to Harvard students but as its social advantage was realised, it was expanded to other colleges in the Boston Area, Ivy League, and Stanford University.

Opening peoples' mind to what is known as social networking, wherein people can build a personal profile and connect with friends across the planet, TheFacebook easily earned widespread attention from numerous audiences. A few months after it was launched, its expansion continued and it quickly became a growing phenomenon; gaining American colleges while gradually reaching most of the universities in Canada. TheFacebook expansion was so fast and trending that in a matter of months, it had gained 8 million users in the United States alone and was already expanding to seven other English-speaking countries. In 2005, TheFacebook dropped the word "The" from its name after moving its base operation in California and purchasing the domain name of facebook.com.

Back then, Facebook was limited to building personal profiles and viewing others' profiles, sharing stories through statuses and commenting on others, and connecting with friends. Its blue pages were made simple but its live chat features enticed more people to join, somehow outliving Friendster and MySpace. During the first few years of existence, the frictionless story sharing on Facebook led to numerous privacy and safety concerns among users. It was later discovered that kids as young as 13 years old were abusing its security settings. The use of obscene language and violent photos have also caught the company's attention, prompting them to build sturdier Facebook features and controls.

In March 2011, Facebook removed approximately 20,000 profiles from the site as part of a regular clean-up for various infractions, spams, inappropriate content, and underage memberships. In response to the plight of members for more secure and organised story sharing, Facebook finally rolled out its 'Timeline' view in 2011. With a more refined privacy setting and enhanced user control options, Timeline made each user's Facebook experience even more fun and tenable.

From a simple college platform, Facebook has now become a worldwide phenomenon infecting billions of people with the positive (and negative) impacts of social networking. Since Facebook was launched in February 2004 however, it has changed enormously (along with its users). Facebook originally provided a variety of exciting features, which gradually added support to students in other universities. The basic yet exciting features included: being able to chat while online, receiving news feeds from friends within the network, connecting with friends, commenting and liking relevant statuses, and of course, creating pages. Along with other developments and add-ups, Facebook's popularity finally spread throughout the world, faring better than MySpace and Friendster, two alternative social networks that were also widely used at the time.

In December 2011, Facebook replaced Facebook Profile with Timeline, a new virtual space which provides users with more exciting features. With the new Timeline, users are able to upload and categorise photos, videos, and posts according to the period of time in which they are created.

In a 2012 survey, Facebook Pressroom recorded over 1 billion active users, 200 million of which come from the United States alone, while 50% of which are active users who log on to Facebook every day. From a simple school platform, it has become the largest social networking site, which currently plays an integral role in people's daily activities. Aside from being merely a social network, Facebook is now considered by many as an effective channel to market goods and services. Its global platform has given advertisers the perfect spot to spread the word about their products and influence thousands of buyers around the world. Politicians have also taken advantage of its wide coverage in winning over voters in presidential elections and organising protest movements. As a matter of fact, President Barack Obama used Facebook to get elected. It has provided numerous opportunities for different companies to seek applicants, like Dell, who recruited new employees through Facebook profiles. It has also become the best venue for people to express opinions, vent, and share benevolent experiences by creating pages and cause-oriented communities.

Facebook has definitely made a great impact in the social status quo. Just as Facebook, Inc. wanted to preserve this, it continued to develop more features in Facebook, which do not only aid communications between people, but also allow them to enjoy and grow as an individual of the modern era. Although Facebook is blocked in some places like China, Vietnam, and Iran because of privacy issues, it now has 70 translations making it a popular website despite the regional and language barrier.

Facebook still has a lot more to offer in the near future and these are the things that many people are watching out for every day. At present, Facebook has over one billion users, more than half of whom are using Facebook on mobile devices. With the founder of Facebook, Zuckerberg, as the current chairman and chief executive of Facebook, Inc. the company's 2012 IPO and valuation of about $100 billion is considered to be among the largest in tech history.

Facebook Jargon

From 'Posts' to 'Friend Requests', social media sites like Facebook have created a language all their own that may sound like Greek to some. So before we go any further, the following list should clear up any confusion on Facebook terms. This list is by no means exhaustive, but provides a start for those who are unsure or new to Facebook and all its glorious terms. I don't mean for this list to be patronising, it merely acts as a resource for you to refer back to when reading this book if you are unsure on certain terms.

Add – As a personal Facebook user, you can add or 'friend' somebody on Facebook, acknowledging your connection to them. It's the personal equivalent of Liking a business page.

Cover Photo – This is the image that sits at the top of your profile. There are certain rules about what you can and cannot use this space for, such as price promotions, but you can get very creative with it. How about creating a timeline with key dates or using it to display a great picture of your team? You could even incorporate the profile picture in a clever fashion, so it looks as if it is part of the same image.

Events – This is an app on Facebook that allows users to let friends know about events that are coming up.

Fan – A fan is the equivalent of a friend to a business page. A fan can interact with a page, however the page itself cannot talk directly to the user on his or her wall. This is to stop spamming of users.

Friend –Facebook friends are often very different from your 'real-world' friends. Some people out of principle only become friends on Facebook if they are actually friends in real life, though this could lead to some awkward moments at work when your colleague realises that you don't actually like them beyond the working relationship! Friends on Facebook can interact with each other, view each other's profiles and pictures and see each other's Wall posts, although recently this has become complicated by Facebook's privacy settings, as you can now set which friends see what.

Group – Similar in function to a forum or message

board where the group members can share related content or media. Groups are a great way to connect like-minded individuals, such as networking groups or teams who would otherwise be disconnected.

Insights – This is where you can view your Facebook analytics data. You can get detailed information about your reach and engagement figures.

Like – Liking a Facebook page is similar to adding somebody as a friend. The user will see the page's updates and posts in their News Feed and will be able to interact with the page.

Messages – This is similar to your standard email, apart from it all takes place within Facebook. Messages are private and can only be seen between those who are writing it. Note that this can include more than just two people.

News Feed – The News Feed is what you see when you first login to Facebook, showing you information including profile changes, upcoming events and other updates.

Notifications – Status updates, new photos, Likes, messages, how on earth do you keep up-to-date with all these goings on? Luckily, Facebook notifies you via the Notifications tab. When you're signed in and on Facebook, you may also see these displayed as a pop-up box.

Page – Brands, businesses, even celebrities should use pages, rather than personal accounts. Whilst there are some drawbacks, the benefits are far greater. By ignoring this, you risk having your business removed from Facebook. This entire book is based around your business running a Facebook page, rather than personal profile. If this isn't the case, I'd suggest swapping it (there is a guide on Facebook on how to do this).

Poke – Poking is a feature with no specific purpose. Because of this, and its stupid, and annoyingly juvenile name, I will henceforth never mention it.

Privacy – Facebook's privacy policy regularly comes under the microscope. You can put your privacy settings under your own microscope on the privacy page. It allows you to edit who can see what on your profile. I fully recommend that you at least take a look at this page, just to check that your settings are suitable for your needs.

Profile – Individuals have profiles, rather than pages. Their public profile has since become their Timeline (previously known as Wall), along with everything else visible such as photos and 'About' sections.

Settings – All of that privacy stuff can be accessed in the settings, along with controlling other aspects of your profile.

Share – Facebook is all about sharing, but you can specifically share other people's posts on Facebook by using the share button. This then distributes that content to your friends too.

Status – A user's status is displayed on their Timeline and on their friend's News Feed. Users post messages for their friends to read. Friends can then respond with comments, as well as clicking the Like button.

Timeline – This is where a user's content is shown. Business pages also use the Timeline layout. It allows short messages to be posted, either by the user or business, or by somebody interacting with them. It is displayed in chronological order, with the ability to highlight certain posts.

Wall - The Wall was the space where a Facebook users content was shown. The Timeline has superseded it.

Setting Up Your Facebook Account

It would be fair to say that if you are not yet making use of Facebook, the world's number one social media platform, you are a little behind the times. However, it is surprising how many people and businesses are not on Facebook. This may be because you are not a fan of the platform or of social networking in general, or it may be because you don't know how it all works. For these people, here is a beginner's guide to getting started on Facebook.

Before you can do much on Facebook, you will need your own account and user profile. The way to sign up is similar to the sign-up process for other social networking and online services.

The first step to creating a Facebook account is to go to www.facebook .com. There you should see this screen:

As you can see, there is an easy to follow sign up page right on the main website. Write your name in the boxes, followed by your email address, your chosen password, your birthday and then your gender.

Then, you click the green 'sign up' button at the bottom to get started. You will first come across a page that will give you the three simple Facebook steps that allow you to utilise its services the best you possibly can. The first step is to find your friends. Facebook uses your email address to search its users for common contacts to increase your network.

You are able to skip the steps that aren't applicable to you by clicking the 'Skip' button at the bottom right corner of each box. The three steps provided by Facebook are 'find your friends', 'profile information' and 'profile picture'.

After you finish filling out details of your high school, university and employer (if you choose to do so), Facebook will give you a long list of people you might know that you can add as a friend. Add them by clicking the button that says '+1 Add Friend.'

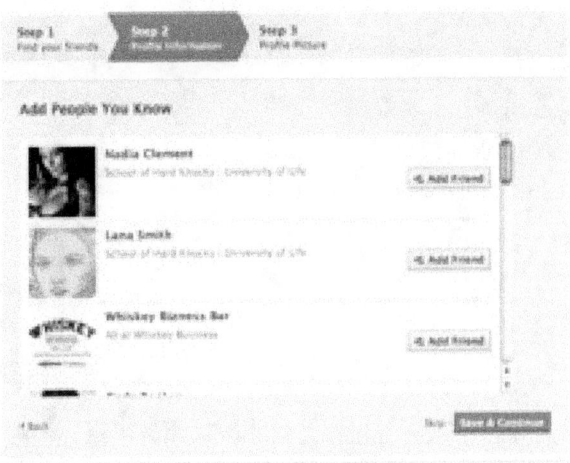

Hit the 'Save & Continue' button when this step is completed. The final step of the three is to post your profile picture. You have the option to either upload a pre-existing photo from your computer, or to take a picture of yourself using your webcam (if you have one).

After you have chosen the picture you want on your profile, Facebook will prompt you to confirm the email address you used to create the account via a notification at the top of your page.

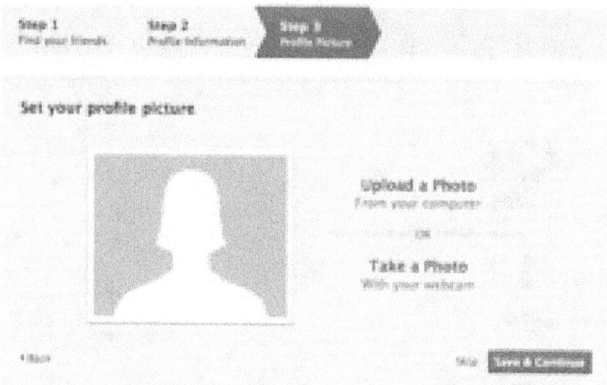

Sign in to the email account you used to create your Facebook account and locate the email that Facebook sent to you.

In the email, there will be a link provided by Facebook that you must follow in order to complete the sign up process and fully utilise Facebook's services. There is also a confirmation code that they might require you to use.

Upon clicking on the link, you will be taken back to your Facebook page, where a memo will inform you that your verification was successful and that your account has been confirmed.

Once your Facebook profile has been created, you can finally create a Facebook page for your business. Go to www.facebook.com/pages/create.php to begin the creation process. There are six types of Facebook pages you can create. These six are;

- Local Business or Place
- Company, Organization or Institution
- Brand or Product
- Artist, Band or Public Figure

- Entertainment
- Cause or Community

'Local Business or Place' is the first option. That is the one you should select to create a small business page.

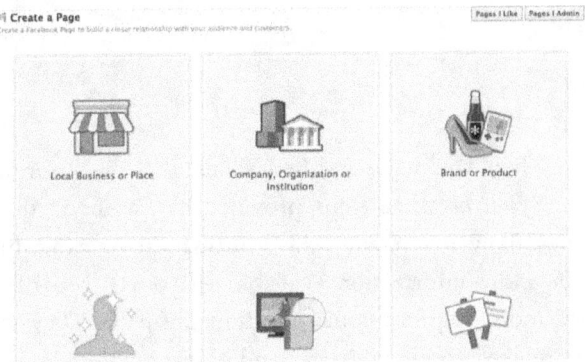

When you click the box that says 'Local Business or Place', Facebook will provide you with the boxes needed to fill out your business information. This can't be changed, so try not to make any mistakes or you will have to start over.

Select the drop down menu to choose the category your business falls under. Then fill out the rest of the information in the box. Make sure to agree to the 'Facebook Page Terms'. Then you can click the blue button to get started.

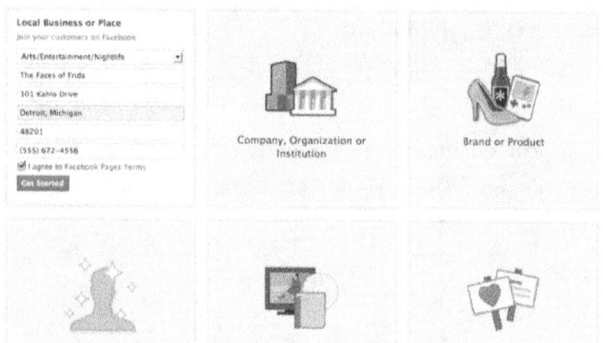

When you have finished filling out the information, there will be three steps provided by Facebook that you can follow to enhance the information on your profile. The more information available on your Facebook page, the more helpful people will find the page. They will be more likely to Like the page and pass it on.

The first step is posting the picture that you want to be the face of your business page. Choose this carefully. You can either upload the picture from your computer or bring it in from your website.

When it is selected, hit the blue button that says 'Next'.

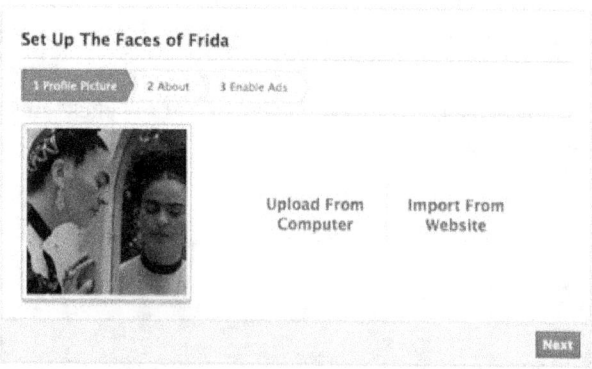

The next task is to write the 'About' section of your business page. You should provide information about your business and a description of its services. Facebook also gives you the option of including other websites that link your business to your Facebook page; this improves traffic and makes it easier for your clients to seek new information.

When you have completed writing your business description, save and move on to the last step.

The last step is enabling ads. Most businesses will want to do this because enabling ads will bring in a little more money. Just make sure you have some kind of credit or debit card number attached to your profile and Facebook will advertise your business for a small fee. In turn, this will bring you more customers by spreading the word about your business virtually to millions of people.

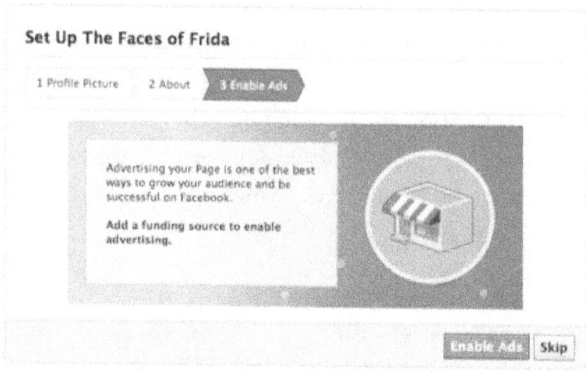

When you are nearly done with the creation of your page, Facebook will have a few last prompts for you. The first is to Like your business page. This enables visitors to your page to see that someone else has Liked your services and will encourage them to Like it as well.

The next prompt is for you to invite your friends to view your new business page. They can show their support for you by Liking it as well. Remember, the more Likes you have, the more popular your page will be and the more people will trust your business. Facebook will also suggest that you invite your email contacts. It is important to get as many people on board as possible in order to get the word out about your updates and events.

Finally, when you are through with inviting people to your page, you can begin to write status messages, promotions and updates for your business. Anybody who has Liked your page will be able to view them on their Facebook homepage.

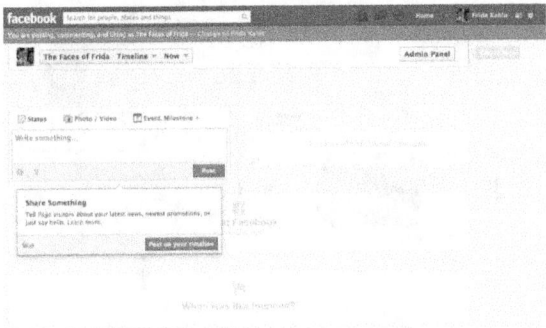

Then you are ready to begin doing business on Facebook with the administrative panel.

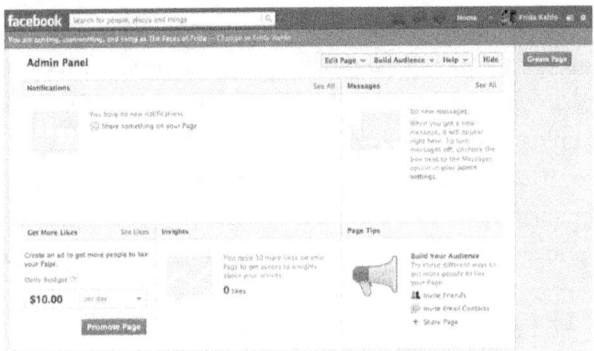

If you ever need to switch back to your personal profile

or from your personal profile to your business profile, go to the settings icon in the right hand corner and choose to use Facebook as either your personal profile or your business profile.

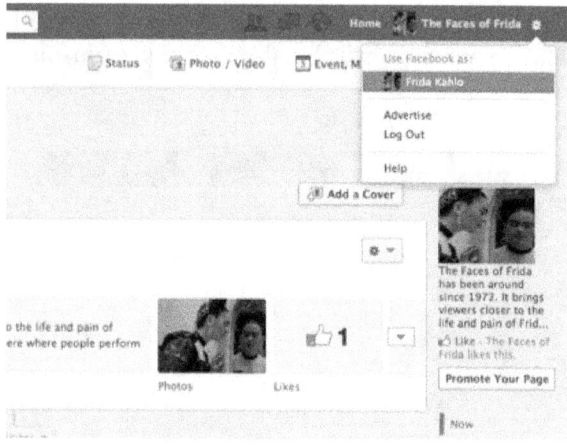

Now that you have your Facebook Page set up, you will need to familiarise yourself with the various admin options. You can manage your business page through your admin panel. It contains various features, which you may use to optimise and monitor your page. The 'Edit Page' button on the upper right corner of the page allows you to update your page info, change your company description, or upload another profile photo or cover photo. You can also use the admin panel to change the role of your administrators; for instance if you have assigned some employees to respond to comments and other relevant queries.

You then need to build your audience by filling in your page with exciting information about your products. Feature in your page your product pictures, product updates, client testimonies, or link to your product reviews. You can also use your business page to alert your potential customers with the latest special offers, events, and discounts. Inviting more fans and contacts to like your page should come after there has been good interaction on your page. The more strategic you are in managing your business page, the larger audience you will gain.

Monitor your Facebook on a daily basis. Leaving it unattended after setting up a page is not enough, as we will see throughout this book. Considering the pace of time, your business page should continue to thrive and compete with other businesses. To check on how fans interact on your page, you can check on the page's own analytics. On the upper right of the 'Admin Panel' you can reply to private messages sent to your page. On the upper left, you can also read the comments from your audience and respond to them. Ignoring these people isn't advised as it will adversely impact your page.

After setting up a page, your next priority should be familiarising the features of Timeline to sustain an exceptional marketing strategy and strengthen lead generation efforts. Depending on the business niche you have, you may create multiple Facebook business pages and drive a lot of traffic from over one billion Facebook users. However, creating multiple pages requires a lot of time and effort and shouldn't be a decision that is made lightly. That's all you need to know about setting up a Facebook account and a Facebook page for a small business.

The Difference Between Pages, Groups and People

Gone are the days of being able to easily explain Facebook's features. In years gone by, when you signed up to the site there was only one type of account, the personal account. Specially designed for individual use, its main purpose was to connect the user with their friends or people they know who have also created profiles at the same time. This allowed every user to get updates of the latest happenings or events of each other's lives without having to contact them every now and then; either through snail mail, email or expensive phone calls. But as business-minded individuals discovered the potentials of Facebook for networking and marketing, it began to evolve into a bigger version of itself. Currently, aside from people's profiles, the network also provides Facebook pages and Facebook groups. So what are these Facebook pages, groups, and people about? How do we distinguish one from the other?

Starting with the most basic, Facebook people (also known as a Facebook profile) as previously mentioned is for individual use only. So if you are a real person and want to connect with friends on Facebook then you can create a profile. A Facebook profile allows you to stay connected and interact with other people very easily. You can get the latest scoops on your friends, send them private messages, tag them to events or pictures and post statuses of what you are currently thinking so that they may also know about it. It's worth noting that these types of profiles are reserved purely for individuals, not for businesses. Facebook does allow you to convert your personal profile into a page though, so if you are currently using your personal profile for business use, I would recommend converting it pronto! Facebook have been known to delete profiles that are being used for business use.

For those of you that are reluctant to change your standard Facebook profile to a business page, the fact that you are in violation of Facebook's terms of service should convince you. Exact wording from the Statement of Rights and Responsibilities:

Registration and Account Security

Facebook users provide their real names and information, and we need your help to keep it that way. Here are some commitments you make to us relating to registering and maintaining the security of your account:

- You will not provide any false personal information on Facebook, or create an account for anyone other than yourself without permission.

- *You will not create more than one personal account.*

- *If we disable your account, you will not create another one without our permission.*

- **You will not use your personal timeline primarily for your own commercial gain, and will use a Facebook Page for such purposes.**

- You will not transfer your account

The next, most obvious point to make is that you'd have no access to all the analytical data that is so precious when using social media for business. What's the point slogging away, putting in the extra hours when you can't even see what kind of effect it is having on your page? Your Likes might not be going up, but your engagement may well be. This is something that can only be seen on a Facebook Page, rather than a Profile. You can also find out who your demographic is, accessing data such as the age and sex of your audience, where they are from, and what languages they speak. This is all information that should be worth its physical weight in gold to businesses!

The final point to pick up on is that you will be missing out on Facebook Advertising. Sure, you're not using it at the moment, but as we will see a little bit further on, it can be a mighty powerful tool to have in your cabinet! How does doubling your engagement for a very small fee sound? Doubling conversions for not much more? These are all things that you will be able to experiment with if you have a Facebook Page.

For those of you that are running on a Profile, I bid you farewell, as this book only deals with Pages, hence the 'Business' part in the title.

Facebook pages, on the other hand, are for public figures (bands, celebrities, and public officials), businesses, organisations, and other entities who want to create a public presence and provide information or updates to fans in an official, public manner. They are purposely made to be visible. Therefore one can connect with them anytime by Liking the page or becoming a fan, and instantaneously the latest news about them will be fed on the subscriber's Wall. The only requirement for making a page is that it should be created by an official representative of the public figure, business, organisation, or entity. Similar to profiles, it also needs real people and names, because once Facebook finds out that the page is not legit, they will remove it immediately without notice.

Lastly, a Facebook group is for people who share a

common interest; be it a cause, an issue, an event, or any topic there is. It is like a forum or message board where the group members can share related content or media. Since it is halfway between being a private profile and a public fan page, administrators have full control on the group's privacy setting. They can either make it public but require approval for persons to become members or keep the group private and invite only those people who they think should be part of the cluster. I use this type of page regularly for creating networking groups and for business ventures with groups of people who might not be connected in other ways. It helps to create a team atmosphere amongst people who would otherwise feel disconnected.

Making Your Facebook Page Look Great

Facebook Timeline gives business individuals everything they need in one easy-to-manage system. With the new virtual space, it becomes easier for users to: monitor their brands and social feedbacks, engage in better customer relations by publishing content across multiple profiles, filter the most relevant information from the hundreds of conversations through the News Feeds, and measure the company's overall effort through Facebook Insights or Google Analytics. Despite all of this, so many companies have shoddy-looking pages.

According to the latest survey, Facebook has become the top most-visited website, with over one billion active users all over the world. Thus, a great Facebook page is crucial to attracting millions of potential buyers every day. Considering the number of potential buyers that can view your page, you definitely need to beat the hundreds of competitors with a great Facebook page. To make your page look great, listed below are some points that you should be focused on.

Adding your company's name sounds obvious, but many Facebook pages don't even seem to have a clear name. You should obviously be using a unique name for your business or company, possibly one that will outline the nature of your products or services. Since your brand name will appear on the top part of your Facebook landing page, it is best if your name is catchy and creative, based on your own original ideas. Of course, you may already have a brand name, in which case I wouldn't recommend changing it for Facebook (more on staying consistent later). Along with your brand name, you'll need to add some information to the 'About' section. There is a limit of 165 characters, so avoid long-winded tales of how you've fought off demons and risen above evil emperors to bring your customers a fairly plain product. Instead, be succinct and to the point. That being said, comedy can really work here, so you may want to include a small reference to demons and evil emperors!

The first impression on any web page is almost always visual, so uploading a high-quality photo that is relevant to your products or services can really help. It can be an image of your products or models with your products, depending on the type of business you are running. By all means, you may edit your profile image before uploading it to enhance its overall impact and be able to bring a uniqueness that will attract viewers. While Facebook requires profile images to be at least 180 pixels, it would be best if you format your pictures to the correct aspect ratio before uploading to avoid a distorted or pixelated image. Along with your profile image, which is seen most by users, Facebook also now allows you to upload a Cover photo. This image sits at the very top of your Facebook page and can create a real visual impact for anyone visiting your page. You may want to consider hiring a professional photographer and designer to create this, although if you're savvy with photo editing you may be able to do this yourself.

Whilst we're on the subject of Timeline, it's worth noting that you can backdate posts. This is great for long-established businesses that are new to the world of social media. Rather than looking like the new kid on the block, fill out your timeline with old images, important dates in your company's history and other such information that can give you the respect and distinction you deserve.

Adding Facebook applications to your page can enhance your page's functionality and can bring quality to the content for your viewers. Using the static FBML (Facebook Markup Language), you can add a welcome tab for your viewers. Through the list of Facebook applications, you can also add widgets that will link your viewers to your blogs or other relevant websites, such as Twitter, Tumblr, YouTube, and many more. Using the static FBML is a little bit further than this book will be going, but if you're keen to learn about it, or find somebody who could do it for you, there are a few links at the end which will point you in the right direction.

Google analytics is a tracking system that will help you know the number of people who visit your page and the places that they came from. While 'Facebook Insights' gives a demographic view of Facebook interaction between your fans, Google analytics provides more comprehensive statistics. Using Google Analytics is also the easiest way to track your sources of traffic and top keyword searches.

To attract more viewers and make fans stick to your page, you should not only maintain a great Facebook page but also a good flow of communication with your fans. We'll cover important information about driving traffic to your Facebook page a bit later, but it's important to remember to interact with your fans on a daily basis by attending to their needs, answering their concerns, and solving their problems. Do not limit yourself to solely selling products, but engage in a long-term relationship with your clients and extend your influence by inviting friends. Lastly, provide a place for your clients to give feedback and suggestions, which you may use to enhance your page and customer appeal.

Using Facebook In Your Online Business Strategy

As the economy gets tougher, business is becoming more and more competitive and cutthroat. To make a name for your brand in such a hostile environment takes careful planning and an effective marketing strategy to make sure you are heard and appreciated. The same planning and strategy will help drive your business forward in terms of sales too. With that being said, for small businesses, multiple advertising and marketing streams are just not possible, so when given the option to choose just a single advertising method to promote your business, what should it be? Well, with over a billion members worldwide to date and laying claim to the spot of top social media platform there is, Facebook has to be considered.

In a recent survey that looked at how small business owners were using social media marketing in their online business strategy, there was a surprising trend towards using traditional marketing strategy techniques alongside their social strategy. Many businesses planned to use email marketing and event marketing with most using press releases to get their message across, as well as using outposts such as Facebook. I think this is an important point to remember; whilst Facebook is on everybody's mind, it's easy to forget more traditional methods of promotion. It's therefore important to keep these going alongside any social strategy you are planning on implementing. Facebook isn't the 'answer' to every business's marketing woes; it merely acts as another place to project your message. Using Facebook along with other promotional techniques will help your business to grow, but to do this you need to make sure you have a good strategy and plan in place. This part of the book looks at how you should develop your Facebook strategy to maximise the impact of your campaign.

Creating a Strategy for your Facebook Campaign

Just joining Facebook and talking to your fans isn't enough. You need a strategy if you want to succeed. Just like we create business plans, sales forecasts and growth targets, Facebook needs a thought-process to work. Creating a campaign needn't be hard though; it's just about setting down your goals and how you plan to achieve them with the help of Facebook. For some, social media is about creating a buzz about products or services. Others use it to keep in contact with their existing customers and add value to their service. By keeping your goal in mind, you can create your campaign fairly easily.

Make sure your campaign offers value to others. A nice trick to creating a great social media campaign is to think of how you can help others, not yourself. The common sayings about social media; 'sharing is caring' and, 'be sociable, like us', are testament to this. Social media is about being social, not about being a salesman, so make sure you are sharing content that is valuable to others. Try to provide information that solves problems that your fans have and offer incentives for people to connect with you.

Of course, you could provide the best incentives to Like your company page, but if the content you share isn't of good quality, you'll have people disconnecting from you just as quickly! It's really important that the stuff you're sharing is of the highest quality and to make sure that as much of it as possible is original. If you only share tech news that is produced by the BBC or CNN, why would people Like you instead of the BBC or CNN? Original, quality content can really define your business as a leader in its field. Creating innovative content is a great way to get people to notice your business. Dull and boring content will be skimmed over, but by having a unique voice, with ground-breaking content, you'll be putting yourself ahead of the competition quicker than you would think.

Remember to give yourself a breather from time to time to keep your creative juices flowing. You might not realise it but a simple Tweet or Facebook shout-out can already be taking too much of your time. It can also stress you out. Just thinking about a clever Tweet or an attention-grabbing status can take a toll on you, especially if you expect yourself to do this several times a day. Worst-case scenario is you burn out and you stop posting altogether. Sometimes, you get a light bulb moment, but you are not in the position to publish it, so you wait until later and then you lose interest. You might end up with random, scattered posts that are useless and irrelevant to your audience. If you find yourself in this position, it would be wise to schedule your posts so that you can have a level of consistency in your social networks. We'll cover a bit more on consistency, and the importance of it towards the end of the book.

Finally, once you've got your head round what you're going to be doing and how you'll be doing it, you need to devise a plan to measure your results. As I've previously mentioned, you can't always expect huge gains overnight with social media, but you do need to track your progress. There are hundreds of tools to keep track of your social media campaigns, from Google Analytics segments to tools designed specifically for social media management and tracking, such as HootSuite. Ultimately, it's about finding the tool that provides the right amount of data for your needs, in an easily readable format, which won't take you hours to compile each month.

A successful social media campaign can often be defined as how carefully you are listening to your users. Feedback given by users is essential to building your campaign, and as such, growing your business. Pay attention to your audience, as they know what they like better than you do.

Draw Inspiration from Big Brands

Social media is the way in which most of the world's populace connect with one another and with companies. This is why marketing for large and small companies has had to migrate to the social media realm. Social media marketing is a form of marketing that all companies, regardless of their size, will need to look into.

As with all marketing mediums, it is the big brands that others look to in order to see the best methods. This is due to these big brands traditionally having had a monopoly on media marketing. It was these big brands that could afford the marketing structures of the past which would reach the same audience as social media. However, is what these brands do in line with social media?

Marketing is about getting people to recognise your brand. Traditionally, the big brands like Coca-Cola and Nike have been able to achieve this. The traditional marketing areas would have been billboards, newspapers, magazines, radio and TV ads. All of these would cost a fair amount to run in areas and at times when they would be seen by the largest number of people. A small business would never be able to compete with these brands.

Not only did the big brands hold a monopoly on the local media, but globally they had no competition. Before the advent of social media, the average small business would never be able to advertise globally, or even outside their own city. It was this control that allowed these big brands to become the authorities we recognise today. It was through the inundation of imagery and marketing that these brands were able to become household names.

So how exactly does social media change this? Social media is one of the ways that the global community has opened itself to the average person; it is now easy to connect with those that live in different countries, regardless of the time of day. Social media has also increased the audience that marketers have, expanding from the population of a city to include the whole world. So, you would assume that with this change in audience and the way media is viewed that marketing would change, and the big brands would be the ones to show the way.

So what have big brands been doing to market themselves to this new type of consumer? The answer is that most of them have gone on the same way as before. They continue to present their brand to people in the way that has worked for them so far. Of course, there are some big brands that have tried to become a bit more creative in order to get the business they want.

Facebook is one of the biggest social media websites out there, if not the biggest. There are millions of people using the site every day. This is the ideal place for marketing, as you have a large audience who are willing to look at different aspects of Facebook. So how are the big brands using this platform to market themselves?

Facebook has fan pages that their users can Like. These pages can be based around anything from a band to a big brand. The big brands are creating fan pages for themselves as their primary means of marketing on Facebook. This is a very good way of starting because when someone signs up for a Facebook account they are asked about things they like. At this point most people will Like the page of a big brand simply because they recognise it. They may also assume that by Liking the page they will be privy to additional information about the brand.

Once the page has been Liked, any update to the page is sent to the user via the page feed link. This will appear on the Wall the user sees. This is the second point of marketing that the big brands use - by updating regularly they are able to have a steady flow of marketing in the form of page feeds. Of course, not all big brands use this to its full potential. Many only update their pages every now and then.

Another way that the more creative big brands are marketing themselves through their Facebook pages is by having exclusive offers. Some big brands will have offers that are only available to people who have Liked their Facebook page. Others will offer competitions that only people who Like their page can enter.

So if this is how the big brands are doing it, should small businesses follow the same pattern? Honestly, the big brands are relying on the fact that people already recognise them when marketing on Facebook. They do not actively seek out people they feel would like their brand and it is all a bit cold. The whole idea of social media is to make the global community more personal.

Small businesses can learn from the big brands only to a certain extent when it comes to social media marketing. Small businesses will have to actively seek out people to Like their pages because they do not have the same recognition as the big brands. Connecting on a more personal level can make people feel more comfortable with the smaller businesses, especially when they don't yet have a reputation to go on.

There are also other marketing methods available on

Facebook that some of the big brands ignore. Facebook ads are used by some big brands and they can be a helpful tool in getting users to fan pages that they would not find otherwise.

Interaction is another option that many big brands forget about that small businesses can excel in. If a user leaves a comment on your page, take the time to reply. This makes the user feel important and makes the whole interaction with the company more personal. The user will feel like you took time out of your day to solely address their concerns.

What small businesses can really learn from big brands is that social media is about the human behind the computer screen. Everyone wants to feel more connected. Using the traditional marketing system of pumping out your image will not get you the same fan base if the information you give them is not something they can relate to.

Driving Traffic to your Facebook Page

Before a company can use Facebook as an extension of their marketing, they have to generate traffic to their page, and this can pose a challenge to businesses that are unsure how to do this. In order to generate traffic, you need to promote your Facebook page. This section details some of the ways to increase the traffic, in order to use Facebook to its full potential.

Your website is a hub of information for your business, and most of your customers will have visited your website in order to learn more about your company. Using a Facebook widget, you can easily inform and link your customers to your Facebook page from your website. You can choose different widgets—there's even one that has a Like box so your customers can Like your Facebook page directly from your website.

If your company sends out email blasts or newsletters, make sure that you let your subscribers know that you now have a Facebook page. Again, you can use widgets that allow you to send these individuals directly to your page, which will generate traffic. Another good idea is to make sure that you add content before your widget, to tease your subscribers about what they can find on your Facebook page. Knowing what your page has to offer will entice them to click through.

Chances are you send a great deal of emails on a weekly basis, and like most businesses, you probably have your contact info placed in your email signature block so your customers can easily get hold of you. Think of your Facebook page as an additional contact method, and add a link to your Facebook page in your email signature. This puts a link to your page in front of anyone who reads your email, whether or not they are already a customer.

Many companies are using contests through Facebook in order to generate traffic to their page. This is a great way to get your company name out there and build a fan base. Your contest can be something lengthy that contains a phenomenal grand prize, or it can be something smaller that occurs on a weekly basis. You can hold a photo contest, ask trivia questions, have your customers make suggestions on products—anything can be turned into a contest, and as long as it is run smoothly and follows the Facebook guidelines, you will easily see a jump in your Facebook traffic.

You can use a portion of your marketing budget to invest in Facebook advertising, in which an ad for your company's page will be placed on Facebook, allowing current and potential customers to learn that you have a page and Like it. Facebook ads allow you to reach your target audience within your own budget, and it's a great way to generate traffic to your page. There's more on Facebook advertising in the next section.

Once you've made a great Facebook page, use these tips to boost traffic to your site and generate a large fan base. Just make sure that once you have these fans, you continue to generate engaging content in order to keep them.

Using Events to Promote Your... Event

Facebook Events is an app on Facebook that allows users to let friends know about events that are coming up. Friends use them to publicise birthday parties and gatherings, naïve teenagers use them to announce their house party details to the world and professionals use them to discover networking events in the local area. These events can be 'Public' or 'Private', something that teenagers organising house parties rarely know, and can detail location, start time and even a guest list of who's going, something that teenagers organising house parties always know. Private events are found by invite-only, whereas those that are public can be seen by anybody. So public events are often used by businesses to promote their own events. From shop openings to grand sale days, events are a great way to spread the message about any interesting events you've got planned. They are a great way of connecting with your fans and target audiences, inviting them to events and getting the event into the social-sphere.

Of course, just like everything on Facebook, you can't just dive in and create an event, expecting thousands of people to attend. You need to plan your strategy carefully, drafting out how you intend to promote the event and your timeline for doing so. Sending out invites should be the first thing on your to-do list after you've created the event. By inviting all your friends, you can jump start your campaign by asking those closest to you to attend. Of course, don't go spamming your personal friends with business requests. If your best friend doesn't like fashion, don't invite them to your fashion show that you are planning to launch your new clothing store at. Instead, pick those friends who are actively interested in what you do. By picking those who are more likely to attend, your event will have a stronger 'Attending/Maybe/Not Attending' (AMN) ratio. This information is displayed to all invited guests and because, as humans, we all like to follow the crowd, a high number of 'Not Attending' guests may signify that the event is not the sort of place most people would be seen at. Getting a great AMN ratio early on will actually make your event more attractive to invitees.

Once you've invited your friends and you've given them a couple of days to respond, it's time to spread the word to the rest of the world. Start on Facebook by 'Sharing' your event with the fans on your page. Again, give them a couple of days to respond before moving onto the next platform. Now is a good time to start to incorporate other methods of promotion. Stepping out of

Facebook will allow you to attract fans that are not currently connected with you. If you've got an email list, create a mailshot with a tool such as Mailchimp. Setting up a mailing list is easy and involves minimal cost – you can then use it to promote your events. This goes for other outreach tools such as blogging and Twitter.

You don't need to exert blood, sweat and tears to promote your event however. You can utilise social adverts directly on Facebook too. Every time somebody RSVP's on your event, their name will also appear alongside your advert, making it a lot more enticing for their friends. Facebook advertising is covered in a bit more detail further on in this book, but it's worth knowing that this is an option. It's also worth knowing that I have ordered this section of the book into the order in which you should promote your event. That is, invite your personal friends first, then your Facebook fans, then step out of Facebook; targeting those who already interact with you and your brand, finally targeting people who don't know about you or your brand through Facebook advertising. The reason for this is simple: growing an event slowly will make it easier for you to keep on top of questions asked within the event and keep your AMN ratio looking great!

When your event gets a bit closer, you may want to send out a reminder about the event. People lead busy lives, and although many seem to be constantly connected to Facebook, some of us only check it once a week. Your fans might forget what they RSVP'd to or simply when it was. A friendly reminder will drive the rate of attendees up no-end, but be careful not to spam your fans. You might have an event on every weekend, but I'd recommend thinking carefully about inviting every fan, every week to these events. You'll very quickly lose your fans if they aren't interested. This brings me to remind you about the restrictions of geographical location. Yes, where a fan lives is going to have a big impact on whether or not they attend your event. Online, you may have fans and customers from all over the world, but are they really going to be able to attend your event in the rolling British countryside?

Converting Facebook Users

With the largest number of users around the world, Facebook poses a great opportunity for many business owners to gain a lot of customers. By using a good marketing strategy, it is easy for you to convert active audience into highly engaged website visitors.

Converting Facebook users to loyal customers does not only entail posting ads, creating tons of posts, and uploading hundreds of pictures. After hitting the Like button, it is not uncommon for most fans to not come back at all unless they have good reason to. In converting Facebook users, your first goal should be to give potential customers a reason why they should love your business page.

Hard selling may suggest a lack of creativity and induce boredom in potential buyers. Upon seeing the same phrases, such as 'Work from home, earn extra money! Click here' or 'You are the last winner for today, click here,' customers would no longer want to visit something that is not unique, or is just churning out the same content as other sites. To convert Facebook users to regular customers, you should be focused on three things: adding value to your network, boosting credibility, and building trust through a competitive campaign. It is important to make a point - you are not just selling your products, but you are also willing to give back to your customers by providing them with valuable information, maintaining good relations, and sustaining good page interaction.

Don't just collect Facebook fans like trading cards. To convert them into avid buyers, you need to give them reasons why they should become one. Make them feel that they are a part of your network by giving incentives, such as free coupons, free samples, or free eBooks. Make your business page even more engaging and enticing by celebrating milestones, hosting games, sending 'thank you' e-mails to regular visitors, and trying out sponsor stories whenever applicable. You can also highlight positive testimonies and feature compelling photos from fans to show that you place customer happiness above gaining a profit. The more you give back, the more Facebook visitors will come back and stick to you.

Unlike hard selling, tagging on a call-to-action gives room for creativity. Connect with your visitors and convert them to loyal customers through a combination of call-to-action and offer variations, including enticing content, appealing design and style, and easy accessibility. Make your call-to-action scheme concise, engaging, and clear. Letting your fans know what is available for them right on your business landing page will motivate them to explore your page and check on your products.

Find the right tool to measure your Facebook stats; most preferably the one that can integrate online and offline shopping channel information, measure your weekly or monthly progress, and assess your competitor's progress as well. You can also experiment on data mining and data analysis to have a comprehensive report in measuring your progress. Updating your records on a daily basis will help you know the number of people visiting your page, the number of fans converted to customers, and the number of purchases which are crucial to rate your conversion progress.

When converting Facebook users to customers, it is important to maintain close brand monitoring and sustain a good marketing strategy to uphold the desired results. In order to know which method works best for your brand, try these tactics and measure your business page's effectiveness. Take your Facebook marketing strategy to a whole new level one step at a time.

Edgerank Explained

There are numerous studies showing that visitors spend a significant percentage of their Facebook time in the News Feed (around 40% and more). In comparison, only about 12% of time is spent on brand pages and profiles. It means all business owners who wish to present their companies on Facebook need to learn how to increase their EdgeRank and generate maximum reach on users' News Feed. EdgeRank may be confusing and complicated, but it's important to understand how it works.

Facebook promotion and marketing more and more depend on the News Feed. EdgeRank is the algorithm that Facebook uses to determine what will specific users see in their News Feed.

What is EdgeRank?

EdgeRank is an algorithm developed by Facebook with a specific goal or determining what is displayed (and how high) on users' News Feed. The News Feed is unique for the each user and it takes several factors into account.

EdgeRank has its official formula that defines the sum of all Edges. An "Edge" is everything that happens on Facebook, such as comments, likes, shares, status updates, and more. Basically, any action that happens within Facebook is an Edge.

The purpose of EdgeRank is to rank edges in users' News Feed. EdgeRank simply takes all Edges that are connected to the User in question, calculates the EdgeRank and ranks each Edge based on the importance to this User. Generally speaking, objects with the highest EdgeRank will be placed on the top of the News Feed. There is also a small factor of randomization, but EdgeRank itself is the most important factor that determines how an Edge (action, object) will be placed on an user's News Feed.

To calculate the EdgeRank, Facebook uses three factors: Affinity, Weight and Time Decay. They all contribute to the final EdgeRank for a specific user. There are also certain methods that Facebook uses to adjust the parameters that are not available to the public, but generally speaking, these three factors (affinity, weight and time decay) are what determines EdgeRank.

The Parameters

EdgeRank takes three parameters into account:

• Affinity. This is a one-way relationship between a User and an Edge. For example, if a User A interacts with a certain page or user a lot, said page or user will have a high affinity for User A. Similarly, if User B doesn't interact with the page at all, it will have a low affinity for them. Affinity is built through interaction such as commenting on the page, liking posts, sharing content, clicking, messaging, and more.

It's important to remember that affinity is one-way relationship: just because User A interacts with User B by liking their posts or commenting on their pictures doesn't mean User B has a high affinity (interaction) with User A if they don't reciprocate. This is important for businesses to remember, because it means interacting with clients (say, by commenting or liking their posts) won't bring the page's affinity up unless the users reciprocate.

In addition to this, affinity score measures not only a User's actions, but also their friends' actions and their friends' actions. Not all friends and friends of friends are valued equally. For example, if a User interacts with Friend A more than with Friend B, the actions of Friend A have more influence to User's affinity score than actions of Friend B.

• Weight. This parameter determines the value of any specific action within Facebook. All values are assigned by Facebook. For example, comments have a higher value (weight) than likes. Generally speaking, the longer it takes for a user to complete the action (Edge), the more value (weight) it has.

Also, new Facebook features have a higher weight in order to promote these features to users. For example, after Facebook Places were introduced, they carried a lot of weight which made users' News Feed full of notifications about Places. After a few weeks or months Facebook decreases the weight of new features to the more appropriate level.

• Time Decay. This parameter refers to how long the edge has been alive. Older Edges are less valuable than the new ones since they are seen as "old news". This is made to ensure that a user's News Feed will always be full of recent items. However, Time Decay is not the same for all users. Less active users who log in once per week will probably receive items that are a few days old while more active users who visit Facebook several times a day will receive only the latest items.

The Importance of EdgeRank

Theory and mathematics behind EdgeRank may seem complicated, but its impact is easy to understand: if your brand page has low EdgeRank items, then your page updates will be seen by less people. For these reasons, business owners should make an effort to optimize their content for EdgeRank in order to increase exposure.

Some brands have naturally high EdgeRank due to wider media exposure and engaged audience. These may be factors you can't control. Therefore, you should focus on what you can control, that is, creating interesting, intriguing content users will want to like and share and thus improve EdgeRank of your items.

The reality is that many of your Facebook fans probably never see your status updates due to their poor EdgeRank. Facebook tries its best to deliver content in the

News Feed that users will find interesting and engaging. If your content ranks poorly it will probably never be displayed on most users' News Feeds.

One question that needs to be asked is how effective EdgeRank truly is. This is just an algorithm, so how well can it predict what a certain user might like to read about? Turns out EdgeRank is surprisingly effective in choosing what content to display. In fact, early EdgeRank was so spot-on that users found it eery how well Facebook knew what they were interested in. To eliminate this discomfort, a randomizing factor was introduced. As a result, today's News Feed is slightly randomized.

Optimizing content for a better page rank is a reasonable effort, but it must be noted that you can never be in a control of your page rank. First of all, parts of algorithm are kept secret, and also, you can never be sure about a certain User's affinity (and their friends' affinity) towards your page. The only thing you have control over is your content.

Optimizing your content to gain more exposure basically means making your content interesting for more people. You can hope this will provoke them to like and comment, share and click on your links, which will increase their affinity and make the EdgeRank go up for as many users as possible so your status update or a message can appear on their News Feed.

Generally speaking, "call to action" works best into provoking users to interact with your page. Ask them to offer their opinion or vote yes/no on a question you ask. Post an intriguing description of your video that will make people click on it. In certain circumstances, it's even appropriate to politely ask for likes: "Click 'like' if you are interested in our newest product". These methods may seem basic but they can lead to more people interacting with your page and its content, which will in turn make your items more popular and you'll be able to reach a wider audience.

Facebook Advertising

Being the world's largest social networking platform doesn't come cheap. Over the years the creative geniuses behind Facebook continued to innovate and create interactive features on the network which allowed people to make their thoughts and ideas known to the world. Financing such a huge network has always been challenging. Social networks that require payment from the user rarely work well, but littering sites with adverts are just as much of a turnoff. The team at Facebook have worked hard to allow advertising to boost their revenue, but at the same time minimise distraction to users. Of course, if every user ignored every ad, nobody would advertise on Facebook. Therefore, the social giant has been quietly placing adverts in clever places and targeting them to the right audiences, so paid advertisements blend effortlessly into the rest of the content from friends and family.

Facebook advertising started in August 2006 when they signed a three-year contract with Microsoft. The agreement allowed the Microsoft Corporation to place international ads on the social network in exchange for revenue split. This move turned out to be successful - by the last quarter of the year 2009, Facebook announced that cash flow had finally turned positive for the first time. This meant that consumers could continue to use the site for free, with the ads bringing in billions of dollars annually – enough to sustain the Facebook team who continue to maintain the social network.

Facebook advertising has really helped small and local businesses recently, allowing them to target specific groups of people or those who live in a certain area. Anyone can start their own business nowadays and not worry about how and where to start selling their products or services. As a foundation, they can sign up for a Facebook account, amass some friends or followers, and *voila*, business is good to go. This section of the book looks a bit closer at the types of Facebook advertising, allowing you to work out which, (if any) would be great for your business.

But before we go any further, what can Facebook advertising do for businesses? Will it actually benefit your sales and commerce? Well, like the advertisements consumers were exposed to back in 2006, Facebook ads have changed little. They are however arguably better than more traditional forms of advertisements and online 'banner' ads, both for consumers and businesses. The first reason for this is because they occupy slightly larger screen real-estate than other types of web advertisement, thus giving more exposure and details to its readers and increasing the chance of turning them into leads. Second is that aside from the information, businesses are allowed to include their logos or images on the ads, making it attention-grabbing, if not recognisable. Lastly, before they are broadcasted, the company who owns the advertisement gets to specify the characteristics of their targeted audience. Using this, Facebook gathers information from their database, finding the users who fit the given criteria, and then showing it to them on different occasions. Because the advertisements are in their area of interests, the possibility of them clicking on the ad is high.

Sounds good, but how much will a business need to spend to run an advertisement campaign on Facebook? Well, there is actually no definite value when it comes to this, because the amount you pay solely depends on how much you are willing to spend. First you will have to determine if you want to pay per click (CPC) or pay per 1000 impressions (CPM). Then the network will ask for further details about your campaign, before providing you with an estimate of the cost. With CPC, the average fee is only £0.20 per click. But depending on the bids, how huge your advertisement and campaign is, and its click-through rate (CTR), you will either pay more or less than the approximate calculation. Once the deal has been made, the advertisements will then be made visible to identified users at the right upper side of their Facebook accounts.

Lastly, Facebook advertisements are classified into two distinct formats: the first is the standard Facebook ad and the second is the Facebook sponsored stories. Both kinds can be featured on the user's Facebook profile for a fee, but they do differ slightly. That's what we'll look at in the next section.

Before we get there though, I'd like to offer some words of comfort for anybody who's scared by the 'A' word. Advertising is the one word that scares all small business owners it seems. The more I talk to people, the more I realise that they're scared of advertising, especially online. They either think it's going to cost thousands of pounds or it won't produce any results. Of course that is possible. You can spend thousands of pounds on advertising and yes, if done badly it might not produce results. However, done well, advertising online can be extremely lucrative.

Adwords is perhaps the most well-known online advertising platform. It allows you to place adverts on the Google search networks. Predominately this means that you appear for certain key words on Google. You pay a small price, normally pence or cents to appear for certain key words that you define. You only pay when your link is clicked.

What this means is that you're only paying for qualified leads that are actively searching for your product or service.

If you're a plumber, based in Manchester, one of your key words could be "plumbers in Manchester". You could bid 50p for that key word and if someone was to search and click on your link you would pay Google 50p. However, that person then might convert into a paying customer who might pay £50.00 for a boiler service or £2,000.00 for a bathroom refit.

The same goes for Facebook advertising. So let's take a look at the options available on the social network.

What's the Difference Between an Ad and a Sponsored Story?

Facebook ads are not much different to the other ads you see posted (all) over the Internet. These adverts are what give the social network's users free access to use Facebook. So, how do Facebook ads work?

It's simple. A business designs their ad and uploads it to Facebook. They point out what specific groups of people they want their ad to be shown to by using demographic targeting and then pay Facebook for its publication and distribution. Consequently, the social network identifies and pairs the ad to users they think conform to the client's given criteria and only flashes it to them on the right side of their Wall. Now it's up to the user to check out the ad, or if they don't like it, they always have the option to close or dismiss it by clicking on the 'close' icon provided at the very top of the ad banner. But how about sponsored stories? Many tend to confuse them with Facebook ads. What are their differences?

Sponsored stories are comparable to the News Feeds you see from your friends because you only see them when people you know have interacted with certain pages, applications, events, and even ads. Thus, it is similar to getting updates from friend activities; only it involves some sort of business advertising. A more accurate description for sponsored stories would probably be 'highlighted'. Whether you would be interested in the promotion or not, because your friends have interacted with them, the advert will be highlighted on your Facebook account.

To summarise, both Facebook ads and sponsored stories are delivered to consumers for a fee to the advertising company. This is how Facebook pays their bills and allows its users to use the social networking site for free. Therefore, enterprises can share content with a larger audience by taking advantage of Facebook's billion users. Facebook ads are shown to people who fit the descriptions of the business's targeted audiences. So when setting up an advert, you can target the audience so that your ad will catch the interests of users. On the contrary, sponsored stories can be ads, pages, applications, and events that your friends have interacted with. They're a great tool to enhance your position on Facebook by targeting like-minded people to those who already love your brand.

What are Facebook Offers?

Facebook offers are one of the latest and arguably most effective advertising platforms you can take advantage of when you have a Facebook business page. By creating Facebook offers, it is easy for you to bring people to your business. These offers can be in the form of coupons, discounts, contests, or promotions, which you will post on your Facebook page or send via email to your selected clients. Once your client clicks on the offer, it will direct them to the exact location of the offer.

There are three basic offers available to use; in-store only, online only and a combination. 'In-store only' offers are suitable for business owners with retail stores or physical business locations who do not have online stores. Some businesses may have a Facebook page, but do not necessarily sell their products online, such as groceries and supermarkets. Using this offer, you will have the chance to promote your retail or grocery store online. When a buyer needs to redeem the offer, he or she may present a printed coupon or an email to the staff at your business.

'Online only' offers are well suited for businesses that do not have physical locations and are solely intended to market online. This works well for online stores selling fashion accessories, apparels, and footwear, although it's not just a service restricted to those examples. Using this kind of offer will give buyers the chance to redeem offers online and transact business via the Internet by using coupon codes or barcodes.

Out of the three, the 'combination' option is the most flexible kind of offer. This makes it ideal for businesses with an online store and a physical shop. This can also work for hotels and resorts or travel businesses, for instance in giving room discounts or travel promos. Thus, when a client who isn't close to your physical location redeems a discount for hotel accommodation, he or she can simply claim it online or show it once they arrive at the location. This also gives clients from other places the opportunity to take advantage of your offer, regardless of distance.

The choice of offer can vary wildly depending on the type of your business and your budget. Facebook offers an 'estimated reach', which will allow you to choose the number of people who will see your offer in their News Feed. On setting the budget, you may use the suggested budget on Facebook or customise your own budget. The more people you want to reach, the more money you may need to pay.

When making an offer, the most important things to consider are budget, suitability, and appeal. Before making an offer, consider the total profit of your business. If your profit is too small to make a big offer, do not place your business at high risk just for the purpose of availing Facebook offers. It is also important that you design your offer in a way that suits the type of business that you have. Choose the one which you think is most effective and compatible for your business. Lastly, design an offer that is appealing for the audience. Although your offer may have reached millions of Facebook users, no one would care about a lousy offer.

A good offer should be beneficial for you and your buyers. Consider the great numbers of competitors - your offer should contain the things that your clients want the most, in order to grab their attention.

Facebook offers are only available for Facebook pages with at least 400 Likes. If you have less, you can earn more Likes by inviting friends, or read the section on '*Driving Traffic to Your Facebook Page*' again, to gain more Likes before setting up a Facebook Offer.

Things To Remember

This book has covered a lot of the basics, and as much as I love to think of it as the Holy Grail for those who are new to Facebook, I also must admit that from time to time, things don't always go to plan. This section of the book looks at some common mistakes people make when starting out on their maiden Facebook voyage, and how best to avoid them. The majority of these mistakes are just due to inexperience and therefore can be easily rectified. It's for this reason that I believe the following chapter to be the most important in the book. Some of the information is quite obvious when you think about it, but I have been asked countless times why fans aren't connecting with a page that only posts content about products. Perhaps it's not so obvious. Either way, read the following chapter carefully and take it all in. I promise it will save you money in marketing consultancy fees and improve your social accounts overall. The majority of this section goes for other social platforms too, not just Facebook. Whilst there are differences between how you should post on Twitter as opposed to Facebook, many of the underlying principles remain. Being aware, sociable and consistent are all things to remember on any social networking platform.

<u>Be Sociable</u>

People join Facebook to be social, not to be sold at. The number one mistake small businesses (and big businesses) make on Facebook is 'broadcasting' your messages to fans, rather than interacting with them and providing them with relevant content on a continual basis. The main job on Facebook for your business is to interact and be sociable, not to sell. If your company isn't being authentic, or is just trying to sell directly to a fan, people will see straight through it and move onto someone else's page.

It's sometimes difficult to explain this in a way that is easily understandable, so I sometimes ask people to think of it in a 'real-world' way. Imagine you are chatting to your friends over a few drinks after work. You're sat in a trendy bar in the centre of the city and there is some music playing in the background. You're enjoying catching up with your friends from your school days, when one of the bar staff pops over and asks if you want to buy more drinks. You decline, saying that you're ok at the moment, but may want some more shortly. The bar staff leaves without any further conversation. Then, exactly one minute later, the same member of staff approaches you asking if you want some food. You explain you've already eaten and you don't want anything else. Again, they leave without saying anything else. They come back two minutes later wanting to know if you want another drink. Hang on

- you told them only three minutes ago that you didn't want a drink, why would you want one now? Even writing this is starting to get me annoyed, so we'll stop here by unanimously drawing the conclusion that you wouldn't stay for another drink. In this analogy, the company's Facebook page is the bar and you are the Facebook page's fan. Just like you'd leave the bar, and probably wouldn't return, you'd probably 'unlike' the page, and have no intention of 're-liking' at a later date.

You can see why it's important not to over-sell to your fans. But surely by not pushing the hard-sell, you won't see any gains? Well if we continue to use the bar analogy, how would you feel if, in the same situation, the bar staff were polite, courteous, even sociable? I've been in bars where the bar staff are happy to advise on drink or food choice, listen to my ramblings, join in conversations and even exchange jokes. Needless to say, these bars keep my custom. Now if you applied these principles to your Facebook page, you'd be taking big leaps in the right direction to creating a great Facebook experience for your fans. Provide relevant and handy information - just like the best bar staff will tell me what wines go with what food. Chat to people about their social life, especially if it is related to your products or service industry. You could even go as far as to tell jokes. A joke a week might be gimmicky, but if you could relate it to your industry or products, even poking fun at yourself, you can really build your trustworthiness and authenticity on Facebook.

Many companies want to use Facebook to make more money, but by engaging with customers and providing an authentic, meaningful online experience, people will begin to feel a part of a community and be more inclined to spend with you at a later date. Facebook isn't somewhere to drive quick growth within businesses, but it can help you to organically grow your brand to an audience that cares and matters.

Be Consistent

Have you got a logo? Have you got a colour scheme? Have you got a tagline? Have you got product images? Have you got promotional images? If you're missing any of these, stop reading now... You're still here? Ok, now are they all consistent? Does your logo match or compliment your colour scheme? Does the tagline work well with promotional images? Are your product photos clearly part of your brand?

Your online presence needs to be consistent, especially your imagery. Due to the nature of small businesses and the way they evolve, owners often find themselves with two or more logos that they use, or taglines and promotional imagery that were created after the logo. Try to keep everything consistent, especially across platforms. If you're on Twitter and Facebook, make sure people can easily identify you on both. Don't use one set of colours for one, this is not how to A/B test![2] So the focus here is why businesses should stay consistent with their content and branding on Facebook.

There are three specific things that should remain

---

[2] A/B testing (sometimes known as split testing) compares the effectiveness of two versions of a particular product to work out which one is better. This can be done by looking at conversion rates.

unchanged when marketing your business on Facebook: first is the logo, next the brand colours, and lastly but perhaps most importantly is the relevant content. Logos have been used for years by companies and institutions to symbolise their brand, their message and to represent what they do. This is because it is easier to remember an image, through the power of association, than a name. People may effortlessly dismiss a long and unheard of company name, but with a logo they are more apt to identify and recall it. Just think of the famous golden arches, an image which is of course related to McDonalds, or the distinctive tick mark of Nike. Whether their exact names were printed under them or not, once you get a glimpse of the logo you know what businesses they resemble and what they are good at doing. So keeping your logo consistent is vital to building your brand. Many people use the social-sphere to build brands; therefore a logo that remains constant should surely be at the top of your priority list.

Moving on to the brand colours; you can readily choose any colour you like to be incorporated into the logo and brand guidelines, but with careful consideration and reference. Colour can have a huge impact on how effective your business's logo is. Studies have shown that colours have different effects on people. For instance, the colour red is associated with increased appetite. This is the reason why most food chains (think about McDonalds again) have shades of red not only on their brand's image, but also inside their restaurants. If you wanted to represent your company as environment-friendly or as fun and carefree, then you could opt for green or blue.

Lastly, but most importantly, is the relevant content. Since we are talking about Facebook and social media marketing, relevant content is essential. The more your audience gets from your business, the more they're likely to give back. It will not only give an inside view into your business, but it will also help you to achieve a good rank on search engines and gain you popularity amongst followers who are ultimately going to keep your business alive. Once put together, the logo and brand colours contribute towards the marketing strategy of your business, and by combining this with excellent, relevant, timely content, you can ensure that people will remember your brand for years to come.

<u>Be Aware</u>

Social media is one of the hottest topics in human resources management at the moment – and given the human fascination with information, gossip, and all the latest news, it's no wonder that social media sites have launched into the stratosphere of the Internet over the past few years. They're where our friends and family are – and they're also where our News Feed resides, as well as being the place to catch up with what our favourite celebrities are saying. In fact, if you sat down the average person in front of their preferred social media site, chances are they could easily spend an hour or more there without getting bored. In short, social media has become a big part of our lives. But how does our fascination with all things social media play out in the workplace? Well, for many, it simply doesn't – a recent survey suggests that over two thirds of UK business IT administrators have banned staff from accessing Facebook via their work computer. Being aware of these statistics is important for anybody who wants to engage with their fans. If they are all caught up with work, it's probably not a great idea to try and engage them in deep conversation. The reasons companies ban workers from using Facebook could of course be to do with reasons that are purely practical – some network administrators may not want people streaming video and using up precious bandwidth. The other thing to note here is that the web has gone mobile – so limiting or blocking access from a desktop computer doesn't necessarily mean that the organisation has banned its staff from checking their social media feeds.

Given the statistic above, it may seem at first glance as if business leaders disapprove of social media – but the picture is a bit more nuanced than that. In fact, a recent survey suggests that nearly half of executives believe social media has a positive impact on workplace culture. So it seems that within some organisations there remains a question about whether social networking adversely affects productivity, whereas in others there is no block on its use. Of course, the important thing with social media in the office is striking the right balance. By developing a policy, employers can help ensure social networking is used appropriately. This means, for instance, that employees have a clear set of guidelines regarding what can be said about the organisation.

As the mobile web increases its reach – which it is doing with each new model of smartphone that's released – social networking policies will need to be refined and in some cases even rewritten. Interestingly, one study even suggests that people would take free use of social media in the workplace over a higher level of pay. One thing is for sure – social media has changed not just the web landscape but also the way we express ourselves as people.

Remembering this is important for anybody setting up a Facebook business account. How freely can users interact with you? Are there times when your fans are more likely to engage with your content? The last thing you want to do is be (part of) the reason for getting one of your fans fired!

Troubleshooting Your Facebook Plan

Whether you're using social media for business or for your own personal gain—or even if you're using it for both—it's possible that you may become overwhelmed while trying to stay up to date with all the new networks that are out there. If you're experiencing any of the following frustrations, it might be that social media is overpowering you.

You have too many accounts

If you have signed up for every social media account out there just to have a social media presence, you are going to be overwhelmed. There is no reason to be on every single social network, and it certainly won't automatically lead to more sales at the end of the month. It will take too long for you to gain a following, and you won't find the time to connect with your following on each one. It takes connection, an established relationship and consistency to be able to gain results. You also need to connect to the right kind of people otherwise your efforts might drive awareness, but you won't see any increase in sales or engagement.

You also need to constantly inform your audience with timely and relevant news about your products and services. If you can, try to share information about other things that are not about you, but still relate to your brand and products. You need to give them valuable information so that they can see you as someone of value. I know that value is something that has been repeated throughout this book, but I can't stress how important it is to running a successful social media campaign.

It's also important to be wary of having too many friends and followers. They don't necessarily translate to buying customers. If you take a good look at it, what percentage of these people actually buys from you? This should also be noted if you were thinking about buying Likes. Don't do it.

You don't have a social media plan

If you're using social media for business, it's an extension of your marketing efforts. For this reason, you need to have a plan in place. This plan will help you determine how you want to use social media, who will be in charge of your accounts, and what your overall goal is for using it. If you don't have a plan, you will not have any structure to your use, and you won't know what you want to gain from using it. If this is you, flick back to the section on *'Creating a Strategy for Facebook Marketing'* and read it again. Everything you need to know to get started is there, use it!

Your only social media postings are automated

Automation tools like Hootsuite and Sprout Social allow you to schedule posts and updates for your social media accounts. If you are only on these tools to schedule your posts and are never on the actual social network, you're never having real-time conversations with your following. This can have a major impact on your overall social media success. Social media is meant to be social, not completely automated.

You don't post

Automating is one thing, but being completely obsolete on social networks is another sign that you're stuck. This means that you either don't take it seriously, that you don't know how to access the accounts or that you don't know how to use them once you're on them. There are some resources at the end of this book that will help you through the basics if this is case.

In terms of time, Facebook marketing for small businesses doesn't have to be that consuming. You can have an incredible social presence for as little as six hours per week investment. That's less than one day a week. Of course, in the early days of your foray into the social media world you won't need to spend quite as much time on Facebook. It does take time to build an audience, both your own time, and time in general, but stick with it and you will start to see some real results.

You post too much

If social media scares you, you might feel the need to share every detail about your life or your business through these channels. If your followers know what your employees are wearing, where they ate for lunch, and what time you clocked out, you're sharing too much. Over-posting is a sign that you don't know when to stop, and this is a major sign that you need to take a break.

Don't post for the sake of posting. If you have nothing good to share, just don't post. Avoid trivial posts such as stating where you are at the moment, unless it's an important event that your customers must know. Don't post if you are just going to say that you are in the supermarket or you are looking for a cheap toothbrush. Don't schedule content that sounds like you are trying hard to be present online when you are really not. Instead, make sure you have a nice balance between scheduled posts and spontaneous posts.

You have nightmares about social media

Social media should not take over your life. Instead, you should use it to gain a following and, in turn, follow those who are important to your personal and business life. Use social media to generate awareness about your business and connect with your customers on a more personal level. If you would rather sleep next to a Puma than talk about social media, it's a sign you need a break.

It's all you think about

If you spend hours trying to come up with the best Tweet or post, you're trying too hard. Creating Tweets and posts should not be a time-consuming effort. You need to use it to share relative information that your following will find interesting. If you write and rewrite posts, you're putting too much thought into it, and you need to take a break.

Social media is meant to give you a way to connect with friends and family and allow your business to connect with customers and industry experts. If you find yourself falling into any of these categories, it's a sign that you're completely overwhelmed by social media, and you may need to take a step back in order to reassess your efforts.

Your Business Doesn't Fit into Facebook

While you may be fluent in your own language of architecture or plumbing, you may be struggling to work out how Facebook would fit into your online marketing strategy. Plumbers are one such group of people who often struggle to fashion a Facebook plan for themselves, often regarding Facebook and social media as completely foreign to them. But it is a language that can help you hear conversations about customer needs and even create a way to reach new customers.

For professionals who are used to talking with their tools, getting started or reaching out to a potential client they don't know can be challenging. But once you get the conversation started, it is hard to stop. Thinking outside the box is key in such industries, but to get you started, here are a few ways to dig into the world of social media and heat up the conversation for such sectors.

Joining groups is a great way to connect to like-minded individuals, including customers as well as your competition. These groups are bundles of like-minded social media users, all posting to the same pages, sharing the best practices and offering tips. By subscribing to group updates, you can be a part of a conversation that could bring you more business, or help you offer services more smoothly to a larger population.

Social media not only allows you to tap into the whole world in one place, but it also allows you to grow your home turf, starting conversations on a local level that you may never be able to have in person. The Internet breaks down many social barriers, for example, allowing plumbing contractors to discuss issues with neighbours, and there is no reason why other local businesses cannot use Facebook in this way too. Chat with other local business owners, befriend networkers who may know someone in need of your services, and work to make introductions online that you can turn into in-person meetings.

Once you have created a social media presence and have gotten the hang of posting, it is time to start the conversation. While your social media friends and connections may not be your average customer, reacting to their questions, commenting on posts and starting conversations of your own makes you seem like an online authority in your field. By engaging in conversations online, you can make yourself the local expert in your industry, and that can translate into sales, as friends begin to trust you as an authority on the subject. Don't be afraid to express your opinion. It could really pay off for you in the long run.

Staying on Top of Facebook

There is more to Facebook than simply creating a profile. Facebook allows small businesses to thrive by bringing in leads, opening greater possibilities, and increasing sales. With Facebook marketing being one of the most effective and cost efficient ways to reach out to billions of potential customers, it can be a place where your success story never ends.

Registering to Facebook and creating a profile is not enough to convey to your audience that your product is good. To stay on top of Facebook marketing, you will have to create a good marketing strategy. To start with, you need to learn about time discipline and management. As a business professional, time is a precious asset, so you need to engage with your customers in the most effective way. Create a time management system that will help you carry out the business operations of your Facebook page. Begin by planning out your entire week. You should be able to list all the important things that you need to accomplish within the week. Although other people may consider to-do lists old fashioned, it remains to be a great way to keep track of your weekly tasks.

Next, integrate your to-do list in a time planner or schedule. Here, you can lay out the dates when you will visit your Facebook page, update your status, upload videos and photos, cater to comments, messages, and suggestions, and respond to notifications. It is crucial not to spend too much time updating your Facebook page. Despite your busy schedule, you should be able to give time to your customers and make them feel valued. Thus, your schedule planner will help you keep track of your tasks.

As part of a good marketing strategy that will keep you on top of Facebook marketing, you should know how to use the Facebook features. With the new features of the

Facebook Timeline, you can implement a better system for posting to Facebook. After you have created a post, you can broadcast your content just a little louder to guarantee that you are seen and heard by your target audience. Listed below are the top Facebook Timeline features that you can implement.

- Pin a post – Pinning a post allows you to manually choose a specific status to stay up on the top of your Facebook Timeline for at least seven days. You can choose this feature to broadcast offers, promos, and other significant announcements that you want your audience to easily spot.
- Highlight a post – Highlighting a post expands your status update across the Timeline page. Since it guarantees wider viewing, it poses a great advantage in drawing more attention to the most important content of your page. As a good highlighting strategy, you could highlight good customer testimonials and other posts that promote your products.
- Promote – This new feature from Facebook allows your post to be seen by more of your audience than usual. Once you click on the 'promote' button below your status bar, your post will be prominently shown on top of your friend's News Feeds. The only downside of this feature is that you will have to spend a fee for it, but it does generally guarantee wider audience coverage.

Climbing to the top of your Facebook marketing potential will take time, as it also entails effort, discipline, and creativity - especially when it comes to time management. Nevertheless, once you have conquered your Facebook marketing, you will realise that all your time and effort will eventually pay off. All you have to do is maintain time management and a creative Facebook marketing strategy to maintain your position.

3 TWITTER

The first time I heard of Twitter I was working for a radio station on their breakfast show. At first I didn't think it would be of much use to anyone. You can't eloquently describe swinging a cat around in 140 characters, let alone send a message.[3] Marketing on such a platform then, would be ludicrous I concluded. I quickly realised however that Twitter could allow the radio station to tap into the local conversation. I used to arrive at the studio just before six in the morning, when texts and phone calls were always a bit slow - at least for the first hour anyway. I wondered if we could instead talk to the 'Tweeters'. I was right. Before we really knew what was happening, Twitter became our keyhole to the community. It went on to almost replace texting altogether. Twitter took off and the micro-blogging platform was born. Of course, during this time, marketers

---

[3] Or so I thought!

had worked out how to use it too.

Wherever you turn at the moment it's hashtag this, and follow that. The world is changing, for better or worse. I recently watched a film called 'Craigslist Joe' on Netflix (@Netflix). The premise is that social media and technology as a whole is driving us, as a society, further apart. I think this is an easy statement to make, especially when you take a look around you on the bus, at a coffee shop or even at a concert. We're surrounded by people, yet we choose to interact with our mobile phones instead. Well, yes, on the one hand that is true. But if we look a bit closer, we are in fact interacting with people *through* our phones. The Internet is becoming a far more social place, and the best part is, it knows no geographical boundaries. I can chat to my friends in America whilst writing this book sat in a pub in Derbyshire. This is the future of the Internet, and I feel that we should be embracing its potential fully.

In fact, cry all you might, but avoiding the Internet is becoming harder and harder. Almost all human transactions can be found online, be it relationships or purchasing. According to a recent study performed by Beevolve, on average, a million users have tweeted at least a billion times over the last 3 years. I personally believe that this is making the 'rest of the world' more accessible and reachable than it was. If you wish to have some power and influence amongst the crowd, you need to embrace the Internet and social media.

Five years ago, you could be forgiven for thinking that Facebook and Twitter would just be passing fads. Now, it's hard to justify ignoring them from a marketing standpoint. Here's a quick question for you: are your customers on social media? If the answer is yes, you should be too. Not bothering them every two minutes to buy something, but engaging with them. So why is it so many new businesses don't see the benefit of having a social presence? Some businesses feel that Facebook, Twitter or Google+ may not be right for them, but as potential customers lead an increasingly online life, the importance of having a presence on these sites grows too.

There are no clear statistics on gender distribution, but it's estimated that female Twitter users outnumber male users by 6%. When it comes to age, unsurprisingly, most Twitter users are young: about 74% are aged 15-25, while people in the 26-35 age range make about 15% of all Twitter users. Only 6% of users fall into the 46+ age category. However, these stats may be skewed - users are not required to provide their age, therefore this information can only be deduced from what they are willing to publicly share within their profiles. It's a known fact that younger people tend to be more willing to disclose their age publicly.

The geographical distribution of Twitter users also shows that the website is more popular in certain parts of the world, such as North America or Western Europe, than others. According to the Beevolve.com research, the country with the highest number of Twitter users is the United States: almost 51% of all users come from the US.

Users from other countries make up the other half of all Twitter users. The United Kingdom is in the second place of countries with the highest number of users: about 17% of all Twitter users come from the UK. Australia comes in third place, with 4% of all Twitter users. Other countries in the top 5 are Brazil and Canada, both with about 3% of all Twitter users.

All of the other countries in the top 10 make up about 8% of all users: India (2.87%), France (1.76%), Indonesia (1.43%), Iran (0.88%) and Ireland (0.85%). These top 10 countries have the majority of all Twitter users. All of the other countries make up only about 13% of all Twitter users in the world.

Some other interesting facts: according to the Beevolve.com study, about 12% of all Twitter users have their accounts protected. Also, females tend to be more active and post more tweets. Most Twitter users (over 81%) have less than 50 followers, and less than 4% of users have more than 500 followers.

On the whole then, Twitter is kind of a big deal. Whilst it's not the biggest social media platform out there, it certainly packs a punch, and has been giving Facebook a run for its money in recent months. Social media isn't going anywhere anytime soon. I personally feel that it will only continue to grow. Online purchases will become dependent on social signals; from reviews to Twitter mentions, social media will shape the way consumers buy online.

The power of endurance is apparent when you talk to those who have been actively engaging in social media on a regular basis for three or more years. It's by no means a medium where you can see quick results, and for this reason, the social networking scene isn't for everyone. The important decision to make is whether or not you can invest the required amount of time, over an extended period. Too many marketers decide that Twitter is the way forward, give it a go, even doing it correctly, for three months, but then give up because they're not seeing the return on investment they were hoping for.

A Short History of Twitter

Twitter was created in March 2006 by Jack Dorsey.[4] It was designed as a simple SMS-based social network. Twitter was born inside the podcasting company Odeo and the original project code name for the new network was twttr. Dorsey published the first tweet on March 21, 2006: "just setting up my twttr".

According to Dorsey, the initial idea was to create a software platform that allowed people to track movement within a city, such as cars and taxi cabs, emergency services, etc. However, it wasn't personal enough; it missed true user input. According to Dorsey, this is how the idea of Twitter came to be: he wanted to make an effective instant messenger that would enable users to locate their friends and see what they're up to. There were many good IM services at the time, but they all required computers - Dorsey wanted something more mobile, something users could take wherever they went.

This idea was made possible with the rapid rise of smartphones in the mid to late 2000s.[5] Twitter was effectively envisioned around mobile devices and it followed the familiar and simple SMS concept. The first prototype of the network was tested on Odeo employees for internal communication and it proved to be very

---

[4] I imagine it didn't just happen 'like that', but I've never had the opportunity to speak to Mr. Dorsey about this personally.

[5] The iPhone launched in 2007.

effective.

Twitter was introduced publicly on July 15, 2006. Later that year, Jack Dorsey, Evan Williams, Biz Stone and some other members of Odeo formed Obvious Corporation and acquired Odeo, along with Twitter.com. However, Twitter was made into its own company in April 2007.[6]

The idea behind the network was simple: sending and receiving short, SMS-like messages with a 140 character limit. It was aimed at localised groups, for the purpose of internal communication; however, the service quickly proved to be effective for many other uses, such as sharing short news, sports results, celebrity gossip and, of course, advertising all over the world.

The Big Break

A great landmark - and Twitter's first real big break - came in 2007, during the South by Southwest Interactive (SXSWi) music conference. According to the stats, Twitter usage increased from 20,000 tweets per day to 60,000 during this event. The people behind Twitter used clever marketing during the event: they placed two giant plasma screens in the conference hallways, streaming Twitter messages. This inspired conference goers to tweet their own messages. For this initiative, Twitter staff received the

---

[6] As a total side note - I think it's worth making a note of this – the fact that it is alright to change, to be shaped by the demands of users, to go with the flow, so to speak. Too many businesses nowadays are ruling out exciting opportunities just because they 'don't do that'. Where would Twitter be if Jack Dorsey and co. had taken that approach?

festival's Web Award prize, with a note: "we'd like to thank you in 140 characters or less. And we just did!"

Twitter has been on a meteoric rise ever since. According to Nielsen Tech Crunch, Twitter grew 1382% from February 2008 to February 2009. One of the main reasons for its rapid success was the popularity of the service with mobile devices. Twitter's inception correlated with both the rise of smartphones and the wide usage of mobile devices, and it proved to be a perfect service for those who wanted to use their mobile devices on the Internet. With its SMS-like, 140 character limit, it was perfect for mobile phone users, and it was great for those who wanted to combine Internet social media and mobile devices. Around the same time, during the Mumbai siege, media outlets realised the power of Twitter and started to use it.

Rise to Fame

Another important step in Twitter's popularity was marked by celebrity involvement. The more famous people joined the network, the more 'ordinary' people followed. It's estimated that between 500,000 to 1.2 million new user accounts were created in a few days after Oprah's announcement that she was joining Twitter. Celebrities such as Ashton Kutcher, Ricky Gervais, Trent Reznor, Barack Obama and many others embraced Twitter, which made this service even more popular with mainstream users.

It's estimated that Twitter users were sending about 50 million tweets per day in 2009. This number rose to 65 million in June 2010 and 140 million tweets per day in

March 2011. It's noted that the network's usage tends to rise during prominent events, such as sports events, major world crises or celebrity deaths. As of January 2013, the record for the most tweets per second is 33,388, a figure set by Japanese citizens, who were tweeting about the New Year on January 1st 2013.

Additional Features

Twitter was envisioned as a handy service for sharing SMS-like messages between localised groups. As the service grew though, it was obvious that there was a need for new features to be introduced. These features have made communication and organisation more effective on Twitter.

Probably the most important feature - one which is essential for the effective use of Twitter - are hashtags. The use of hashtags for Twitter was proposed by Chris Mesina, who made the first tweet with hashtags in August 2007. This proved to be a very effective method for creating and following Twitter groups. While not a feature developed specifically for Twitter, hashtags became an integral part of the site.

There have been too many developments to the Twitter service to name them all, but I'll detail the ones that stand out for me. In late 2010, Twitter introduced some important innovations. The most significant one was the ability to see pictures and videos without leaving Twitter, by simply clicking on tweets containing links and clips. Also that year, application developer Atebits made 'Tweetie', a Twitter application specially designed for iPhone and Mac. The application is now called 'Twitter' and it's the official Twitter client for the iPhone, iPad and Mac. Another important redesign came in December 2011, when Twitter introduced 'Fly' design to make the network easier for new users, but also for the advertisers who wanted to gain popularity and promote their products and services. At the same time, Twitter introduced 'connect' and 'discover' tabs. In October 2012, Twitter acquired Vine, a video clip company. The full service is currently being rolled out as of March 2013. Its purpose is (and will be) to quickly and easily share video clips directly in users' Twitter feed. There is a whole section on using Vine at the end, so that's all I will mention about the service for now.

The Current State of Twitter

As of late 2012, Twitter has over 500 million registered users from all over the world, including celebrities, world leaders, companies, professionals, college students and many other socio-demographic groups of users. These users generate over 340 million tweets per day and perform over 1.6 billion search queries. Today, Twitter is one of the 10 most visited websites on the Internet.

Twitter Jargon

From tweets to hashtags, social media sites like Twitter have created a language all their own that may sound like Greek to some. So before we go any further, the following list should clear up any confusion on Twitter terms. This list is by no means exhaustive, but provides a start for those who are unsure or new to Twitter and all its glorious terms. I don't mean for this list to be patronising, it merely acts as a resource for you to refer back to when reading the book if you are unsure on certain terms.

bot - A Twitter account run by a program rather than a human. There are good bots, such as the ones tweeting breaking news from a media outlet. On the other hand, there are bad bots made for sending spam.

direct message (DM) - Also known as a 'direct tweet'. This is a private message you send to a specific Twitter user. The message is delivered to their inbox and only the sender and recipient can see it. You can only send direct messages to users that are following you. If you wish to send a DM via a phone, you should begin your message with 'd username' to specify the recipient. Direct messages also have a 140 characters restriction.

hashtags (#) - These are specific Twitter markings for tags and keywords. You are free to invent your own hashtag (keyword) that other people will be able to use and search. To create a hashtag, simply precede a term with the # symbol. This is a powerful way to tag any subject you can think of. Hashtags are searchable, so all Twitter users (both followers and non-followers) can use them. The most popular hashtags appear on the 'trending topics'. Hashtags are specific because, unlike typical tags and keywords, they are user-generated in real time. Anyone can create their own hashtag, so that other people can search and join the conversation. There is a whole section on hashtags where we cover them off in more detail though, so I won't spoil all the surprises now.

failwhale - A popular cartoon whale that appears when Twitter's servers are overloaded. It was more common in Twitter's early days.

favourite - You can favourite any tweet you like. To favourite a tweet, simply click the star under the tweet. It's also possible to favorite tweets via SMS.

#FF - One of the most popular hashtags on Twitter. It stands for 'Follow Friday'. Every Friday, Twitter users suggest who others should follow by tweeting their usernames with the #FF hashtag.

follow - Following someone on Twitter means subscribing to their tweets. Their tweets will appear on your timeline. It's generally advisable to never follow too many people who don't follow you back, but again, this is covered off in more detail later on in the book.

follower - A follower is a Twitter user who has followed you. Your Twitter messages appear on their timeline. You may choose to reciprocate or not. Having a high number of followers is considered high-status.

lists - A special, curated group of other Twitter users. You can use lists to gather individual users in different groups on your Twitter account. For example, you can make lists for family, co-workers, news, favourite brands, and more. This makes your timeline more organised.

protected (private) profile - Twitter profiles are public by default. However, users may choose to protect their accounts, so that their tweets will be seen only by the approved followers. These tweets do not appear in searches.

@reply - These are public tweets directed at specific people. You send them by using an @ sign followed by the username. When you precede a username with the @ sign in your tweet, it becomes a link to a Twitter profile. These tweets are public, so anyone can see them and join the conversation.

retweet (RT) - This is a message you quote/copy because you find it interesting or important. Basically, you are retweeting someone else's message so it will appear on your Twitter feed with a credit to the original poster. There is a special 'retweet' link under every tweet that you can click to simply retweet a message. One word of warning: retweeting can add characters to a tweet (because it includes the original poster's username) so it may force the message over the 140 character limit.

search feeds - You can use the search box on your Twitter homepage to search all public tweets based on keywords, hashtags, usernames and subjects. You may also perform a search at search.twitter.com. You can also set a specific search feed to track specific searches or to see all messages a particular Twitter user is sending and receiving.

shorturls - Also known as URL shorteners. Since Twitter messages are limited to 140 characters, using a full URL address takes up the necessary space. For these reasons, there are popular services made to shorten the URL you wish to share in your tweet. The most popular URL shortener services are tinyurl.com, bit.ly, snipr.com, vieurl.com and others.

timeline - This is a real-time list of all tweets. Your home timeline shows all the tweets you have sent as well as all the tweets people you are following have sent.

tweet - A Twitter message. It can be up to 140 characters long, including spaces. People send many different types of tweets, from updates on personal life to important world news. All tweets are public unless a user's profile is protected.

tweetup - A real-life gathering of Twitter users organised through Twitter. These meet-ups can be made based on joint interests, location or any other criteria. Specific Tweetups usually have their own hashtags so all interested users can join in the conversation and planning of a Tweetup.

twitter - a network and social media platform made for sending short, 140 character long messages. People use it to share ideas, quotes, news, updates, promotions and anything else they can think of. It's kind of what the book is about.

twitter feed - This is the constantly updating timeline of your tweets as well as everyone you follow on Twitter.

twitter spammers - Accounts specially set up to send spam messages. They usually send many messages to other users and follow many people but have only a few followers themselves. Twitter does its best to remove these accounts.

twitter squatter - Someone who impersonates a popular brand or a celebrity on Twitter. Some squatters register usernames that resemble popular brands or celebrity names and others go as far as faking the 'account verified' icon on their profile to appear genuine. Twitter does its best to remove these accounts as soon as possible.

username - A specific Twitter handle. It has to be unique and has less than 15 characters. This will be used to identify you on Twitter. To refer to a specific username in a tweet, precede it with the @ symbol.

who to follow - A Twitter feature that can be found on your homepage, in the 'discover' tab. This is a list of recommended users generated by Twitter itself, based on the types of accounts you're already following.

Setting Up Your Twitter Account

If you've already got a Twitter account, you can skip this section. If not, head over to www.twitter.com and follow the simple instructions, both on-screen and in this book.

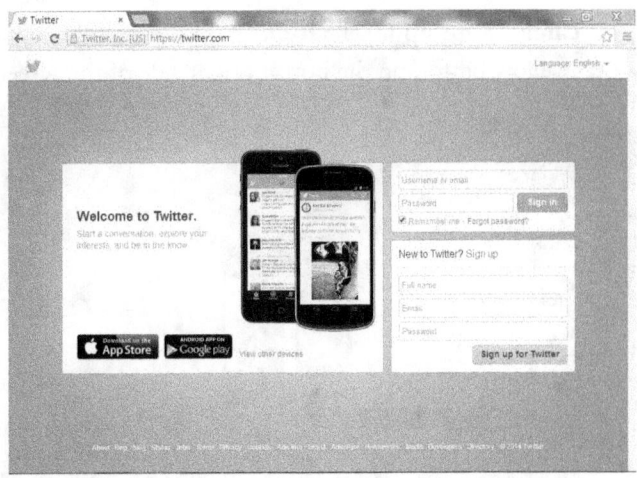

Provide basic information about yourself. You'll need to provide the following information to create a Twitter account:

Your full name, Your email address, Your password (something easy to remember, but hard to guess)

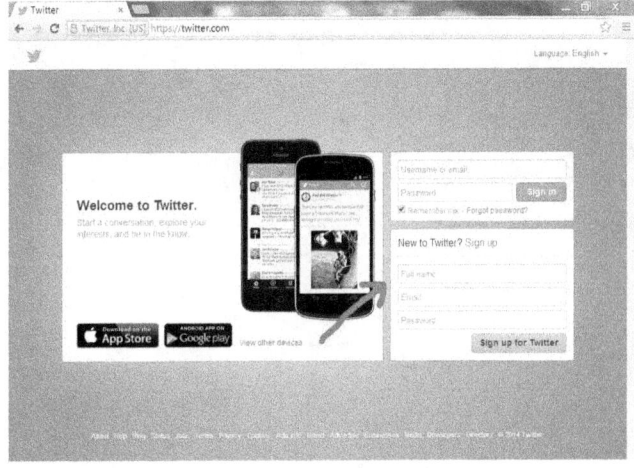

Click "Sign up for Twitter." You can find this option on a yellow button on the bottom right side of the screen.

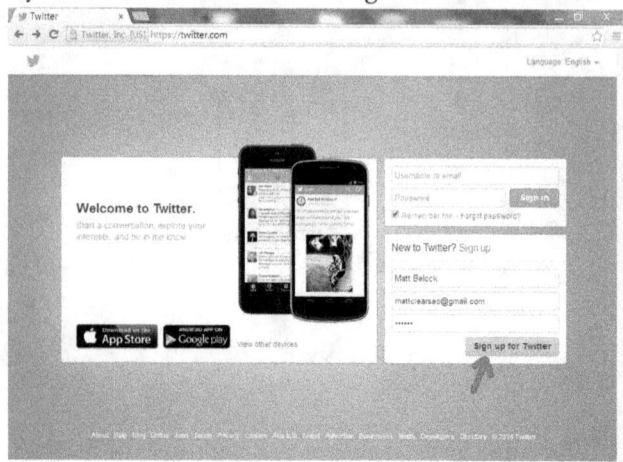

Choose your username. It has to be fewer than 15 characters long. If the name you've chosen is invalid or unavailable, you'll be informed about it. Once you've chosen an acceptable name, you'll see that it's available for you.

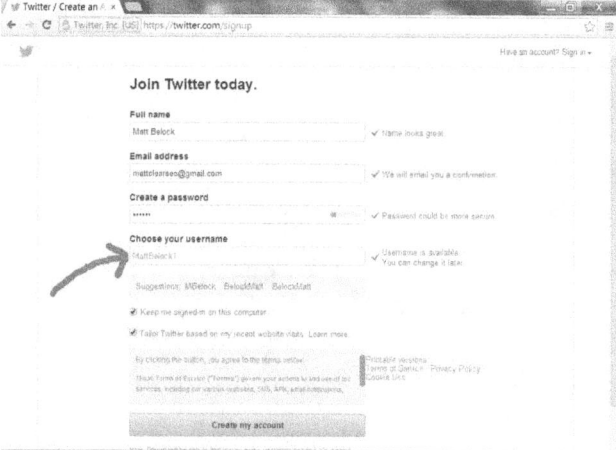

Decide whether you always want to be signed in to Twitter. If it's your own computer, this is a good option. If it's a public computer, you should uncheck the box next to this option.

- You can also choose whether or not you want Twitter to be tailored toward your recent website visits by leaving or unclicking the check mark next to this option.

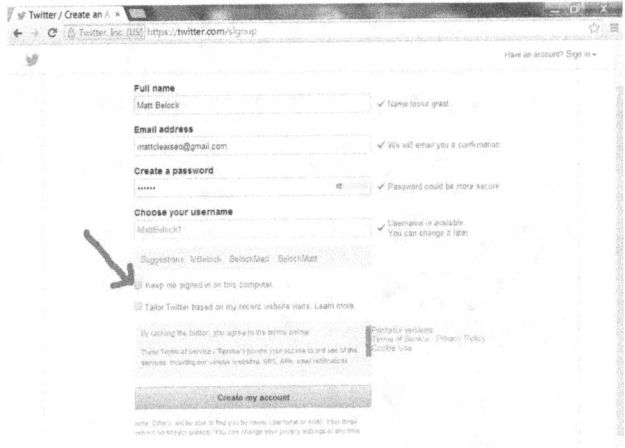

Click "Create my account."

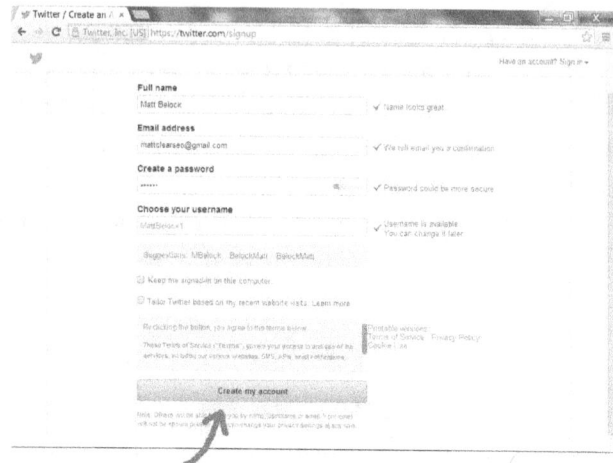

Now You will this this intro window **"Click Next"**

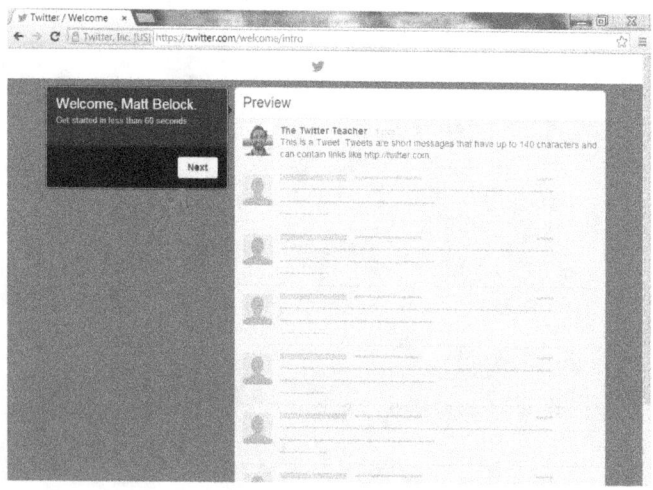

Start following celebrities (optional). First, Twitter will present you with a list of popular people to follow. Click at least five people to follow and press "Next" when you're done. You'll be presented with another list tailored to the people you chose, and you'll be asked to choose at least five more. You can do so and press "Next" again.

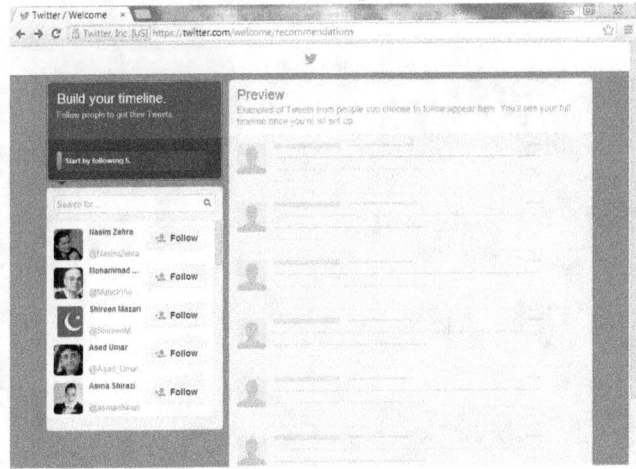

Start following people you know (optional). You'll be given the option to follow people you know. You'll have to grant Twitter access to your email contacts. Once you do, you'll be presented with a list of people you know who are on Twitter. You will have the option of clicking on them to follow a few of them, or even to follow all of them

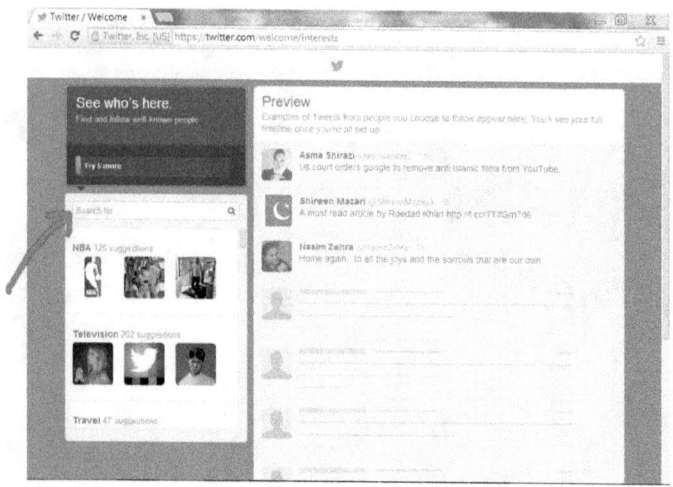

You'll be given the option to follow people you know. You'll have to grant Twitter access to your email contacts This is optional if you want this okay, or just "Skip"

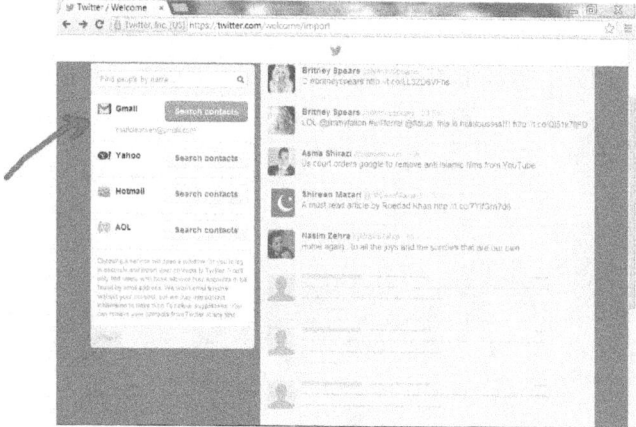

Upload your profile picture. Click on the empty profile photo to upload an image of yourself. Please select a profile image that is less than 700 KB.

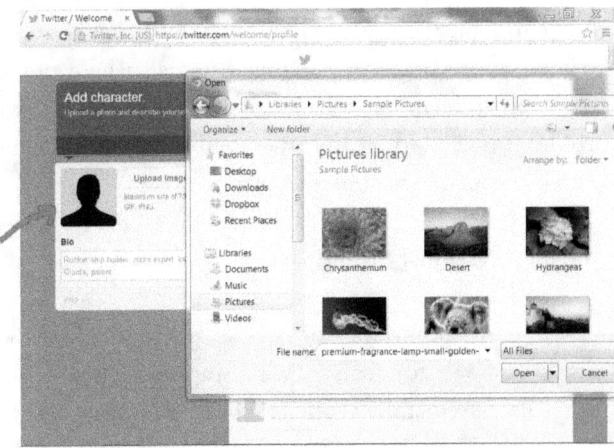

If you haven't Confirm

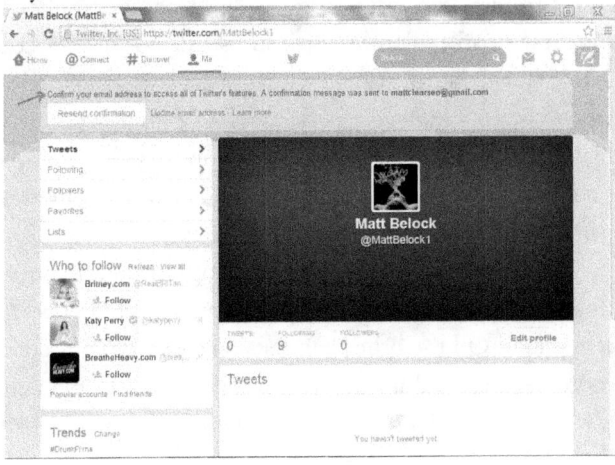

Now you all good to go!

Making Your Twitter Profile Look Great

Building a strong and distinctive Twitter profile for

your small business is very important. It will make your business more professional and it will also help potential customers remember you. To build a distinctive Twitter profile, you need to create a memorable visual presentation as well as distinctive content.

Add a Professional Profile Picture

It's very important to choose a clean, professional profile picture for your Twitter account. This picture makes users remember you and your brand, so it has to be distinctive. This is the first step towards branding your Twitter page and making it unique and representative.

There are two ways to go when it comes to choosing the best profile picture for your small business account. The first one is to use your logo. This is a quick and easy way to build an image representation of your brand and to make potential customers remember your company, especially if you have a strong logo. The other option is to use a photo of a person, usually the business owner.

There are pros and cons to both of these options. Logos are more visually representative and easier to remember. On the other hand, using a photograph builds a more personalised image; it shows there are people behind the company. This may be a better option for small businesses.

Whatever you decide, remember that your profile picture needs to be sharp, clean and representative of your brand or you as a business owner. To me, a pixelated or blurry image represents a company without a clear direction; their own brand is blurred.

Custom Background and Header Images

To make your business Twitter page more professional, you will want to include a customised background and header image. This will brand your Twitter page and it will send a unique visual image to your visitors. Don't forget to adjust the colour scheme to match your brand's colours. There is nothing worse than having differing logos or colour schemes dotted around the web. By this, I don't just mean picking a red for the background that almost matches the red of your brand, I mean you should pick *the* red of your brand. If you're unsure of how to discover the exact colour of your brand to use, it is worth spending a little bit on a designer who can do just that.

You may want to use background images to offer more information about your products and services. With the new Twitter redesign, it can be a bit difficult to include many additional details, but it's important to have a personalised background for your brand. Again, an experienced designer or consultant should be able to help you with this.

A relatively new feature you should also use are header images. Header images are displayed on your Twitter homepage, and the recommended size is 1252×626 pixels. These images help you brand your Twitter page even further. You may include a picture of your products or any other visual detail you wish to emphasize. Some brands use interesting effects by blending header images with the background, such as @DisneyPixar or @officedepot.

Whatever you do, don't forget to include a header image. A page without a header image looks empty and unprofessional. It may also signal that you don't update your Twitter page often.

Building a Strong Profile

Visual representation of your business is important, but content is the key. You should build a distinctive, memorable Twitter profile for your business. Catchy profile text will grab your visitor's attention and it will represent your brand in the best possible way.

Just like all other features on Twitter, profiles are short - you need to keep them under 160 characters. It can seem like it's not enough to represent your business, or yourself, but remember that you may also add other elements to your profile, such as your location or URL. Don't forget to provide this information.

A strong Twitter profile consists of:

- A short description of your business. It will depend on the nature of your business and it should be descriptive and memorable.

- Location. Don't forget to include location information on your profile. Be as specific as you can; detailing your city or at least the country you are based in can add a personal touch for anyone nearby.

- URL. This is probably the only place on Twitter where full URL addresses are used and it will be shown to your visitors. Don't use URL shorteners here; you want potential customers to remember your domain's name.

Examples of Great Looking Twitter Profiles

These companies and brands truly invest into building a strong Twitter image. Their profiles are fully customised and memorable, so they represent the brand in a very effective way:

- Snapple (@Snapple). They use a tagline for their profile description, and they also have a simple but distinctive header image.

- Allstate Insurance (@allstate). The company uses their logo as a header image and they provide additional information in their profile, including a phone number and helpful links.

- Cottonelle (@cottonelle). The company uses distinctive colors and a clean header image to represent the brand. They offer a short summary of their offer in the profile.

- McDonald's (@mcdonalds). The company uses a distinctive background pattern and an image of their products on the header. They also include links to their customer service account and Twitter team.

- Sprite (@Sprite). They use distinctive background and header images. In addition to this, they also include a recommended hashtag for people to use when talking about the brand.

Growing Your Twitter Following, Properly

To be truthful, I was unsure whether to include this section or not. If you follow the advice of this book, you should see better engagement, and therefore a greater return on your investment over time. It will take time though. Whilst many think of social media as an instant platform - and in some respects it is - as marketers and small business owners, we shouldn't be expecting such quick results. Just like building your own social network in the 'real world' takes time, so too does building your business online. How long did it take you to really build up a big customer base for your current business? I bet it didn't happen overnight. That's because very few businesses do actually work like that. We hear stories in the news of the website a fourteen-year-old set up and is now earning millions, but in reality that is only the same as the guy down the road who got lucky on the stock market. For every instant win, there are several slow and painful losses.

So instead of focusing on the instant gains, use this book to implement a social media campaign that will have consistent, meaningful gains. Don't chase the follower count, as it will rarely transfer into more sales.

It's for those reasons I wasn't too sure whether I should even include a section on growing your follower count. After all, if increasing it won't make much difference, surely it's just dead space? But what if you don't have any followers at the moment? I'd first suggest turning to your 'real world' fans and asking them to follow you. Perhaps display a sign in your shop, or add a link to your Twitter profile in your email signature. This way, you're connecting with people you already know and you can start to build your following in an honest, organic way.

Then comes the question, 'how do I increase my followers beyond my ten regular customers?'. Well, paradoxically, the best way to do this is to follow others. By following other people, you will appear on their follower list, and depending on the settings the user has in place, they may well get a notification to say that they have gained a new follower. That's you! Immediately then, you're on their radar. What you then need to do is interact with them. Be social. Your Twitter timeline will start to fill up with their tweets, at which point, you need to interact with them. Replying is the best way to do this. Whilst a retweet can make somebody feel good about the update they just sent out, and whilst it is good practice to retweet other peoples' content from time to time (providing it is relevant to your audience), you're not really socialising with them. Reply to them with something that almost demands a further response. If they tweet a picture of the latest cake they've made, ask them for the recipe. If they tweet a link to a blog post, read it and comment on it.

It really is dreadfully simple. It just demands a bit of effort. Whilst you can find software that can automate a certain amount of this, ultimately if you're not interacting or socialising with others, there is precious little point even having them as followers. If you're not talking with them, you are kidding yourself if you think your followers care about your latest tweet.

Twitter Lists

Twitter lists are a very handy and effective way to organise Twitter users and their content. Lists are curated groups of Twitter users and they help you categorise all of the topics you're interested in. Lists present you with a complete Twitter stream for all the users on the list. They are very simple to create and maintain, and they provide several exciting possibilities for business owners to improve their Twitter success and to offer something new to their followers. Lists allow you to recommend specific people to your followers and they even enable you to keep an eye on your competitors without actually following them.

Creating and Managing Lists

Creating a list is easy. Visit your profile page and choose the 'lists' tab on the left. You will see all of your existing lists and also the button to create a new list. Alternatively, you may click the 'settings' icon on the top right side of Twitter's navigation bar and select 'lists'. When you click on it you will need to specify a few details.

First of all, you should provide a descriptive name for the list. It can be anything you find useful, such as: Family, News, Team, etc. Remember that this name will be used for the list's URL, in the form of: http://twitter.com/username/list-name.

Another thing you will be asked to specify is whether the list is public or private. Public lists can be seen by anyone and anyone can follow them. Private lists, on the other hand, can't be seen by anyone but you. Nobody can subscribe to them, not even people included on the private list. This makes them the ideal choice if you're doing some snooping on your competitors.

Click the 'create list' button and your list will be

created. It's magic. After this, you can add users to your list to categorise them. You can even add one user to many different lists.

If you're more interested in subscribing to other people's lists, all you need to do is to click on 'lists' while viewing someone's profile, select a list you're interested in and click 'subscribe' on the list's page. The best thing about this method is that you can follow lists without actually following individual users. If there is a key figure within your industry, take a moment to see if they have any lists set up. Perhaps they already have a list of great suppliers you could benefit from, or maybe some inspirational tweeters that are specific to your business sector.

You can also link to an existing Twitter list in your own tweets. To mention a list, you need to link to the list's owner and add a forward slash and the name of a list afterwards, so it looks like this: @username/list-name. Also, remember that you can add users with protected tweets to your lists, but you will only be able to see their tweets if you've been approved to follow these users.

How Can Small Businesses Use Twitter Lists?

I've already mentioned a couple of ways Twitter lists open great opportunities for small business owners, but I'd like to take a moment to point out a few more ways lists can be utilised to improve businesses, build a stronger follower base and enhance a Twitter experience. Here are some quick tips for business owners who wish to use Twitter lists:

o   Create a public list of 'Recommended Users' so

your followers can check them out. These can be your affiliates or other users you think your followers will find useful.

o   Make a private list of your competitors. This way, you will be able to track their activity and keep an eye on them without actually following them.

o   Lists help you separate the most important messages and users from everyone else. You will never miss an important announcement or news again.

Organise your interests and people you follow in the most effective manner. Create separate lists for your affiliates, people in your industry, news in your niche and customers.

Tweeting Etiquette

In this section, we'll outline some best practices and things to avoid when you are using social media for your business.

You may have encountered the shameless self-promoter while interacting on your personal Twitter account. You know the one – they're sharing their new blog posts in every other tweet and constantly posting about their latest products. Yet very little of what they promote provides actual value for their fans and friends. It's easy for businesses to fall into this trap because they think they are really getting the word out about their company, but it's a completely ineffective strategy. Why?

Because most people are going to get annoyed and ignore you, un-follow you, and use you as an example of how not to interact on social media.

You should approach social media as if it were a conversation with your customers. It's about providing useful information and asking and answering questions; it's not about posting every ten minutes about your business. I'm not saying that all self-promotion is bad, but it's a good idea to limit it to about 20% of your posts. You are going to get the most bang for your buck if you join the conversation and engage with your customers, rather than try to make the hard sell every time you share something. Focus on content that interests them, is related to your scope of influence, and helps readers solve a problem or find a moment of entertainment in an otherwise busy day.

#Hashtags

Twitter hashtags are a tool that everyone on the social media network should be using. If you are trying to market your business with Twitter then it is imperative that you understand what hashtags are, and how to use them. It is only through the successful use of this tool that you can make a real impact on Twitter users everywhere.

A Twitter hashtag is much like a label or tag on a blog post. This is a method of telling readers about the subject of your post. It also makes your tweets easily searchable through the Twitter search. This is very desirable in the fast-paced environment that is social media. Hashtags usually consist of one to three words which relate to a company, product, person or event. The format of this tag will be a hash or pound sign followed by the label you are using for the tweet. These tags are not case sensitive, but the first letter of the tag is generally a capital letter. Spaces aren't allowed in hashtags either, so be careful when combining words not to create something else. Susan Boyle's media team recently used a hashtag to promote her upcoming album launch, but unfortunately overlooked the fact the #susanalbumparty (Susan album party) can also be read as Su's anal bum party. Slightly inconvenient.

Many of the big companies on Twitter use hashtags when they tweet. The main reason for this is that tweets with hashtags can be searched for easily. Twitter also runs a 'top 5 trending' list on the side of every Twitter user's page. This list consists of hashtags that have the most number of tweets associated with them at any time. Many Twitter users will look at this list to find interesting topics on Twitter.

Hashtags will also help your business by potentially getting you more retweets. The more retweets your tweet has, the more people will see it. This could also bring you more followers in the long run, as every time someone retweets, your original tweet is seen at the top of the search list. This engagement of users will also bring your tweets to a wider audience, as the followers of anyone retweeting will see the tweet.

Big brands like Nike will use their name as one of their hashtags. This helps people to identify the brand and any tweets related to this. When you want to get your business onto Twitter you can try using your name as a hashtag as well. If the name of your business is more than three short words then you should look into an abbreviation for ease of use. When you do this it is best to keep it simple and stick to something people will easily remember. When you are creating your business hashtag you need to make sure it is not already being used. If you use a hashtag that already has some meaning behind it, you could find your tweets getting unrelated traffic. There are a few websites that you can use to help identify the meaning behind a certain hashtag. Websites like 'What the Trend' and 'Twubs' catalogue, identify and describe what the hashtag means, and will even provide a brief history of the trend. Alternatively, you may choose to go down the guerrilla route, and deliberately piggy-back a trending hashtag. Oreo's did this very successfully at the recent SuperBowl when the power cut off. A quick-thinking social media manager seized the opportunity to use the SuperBowl hashtag, and before anyone really knew what was happening (and before the lights came back on) Oreo's were enjoying an enormous amount of 'free publicity'.

When you use hashtags you need to be able to keep track of how they are performing. You can also check on the performance of related tags to see if you should be using them instead. Websites like 'Hashtags.org' will keep track of how many tweets have used a hashtag and even provide a graph to show you the usage in the last 6 hours. If you are going to be tracking less popular tags, then you might have to sign up to a different service such as 'Hootsuite' (more on those services later).

While there are no actual rules about hashtags there are guidelines which have become unwritten rules in the social media world. It is important that you know what these are and follow them. For example, do not overuse hashtags. One or two hashtags per tweet is enough to get the message across. In fact, you do not even need to use a hashtag in every tweet. Many users feel that accounts with overused tags are spam and they tend to shy away from them. Overusing hashtags can also lead to you losing followers as people do not want to be spammed in this way.

Always try and give your hashtag context. If you have invented your own hashtag, other users need to know what it means. You can do this by having one tweet that explains it, or you can have a tag that is easy to understand.

Hashtags need to add value to you and your readers. When you use hashtags it should be done to organise your tweets. You should use them for events, important information or as a reminder.

Do not only tweet a hashtag. Some people believe that it is enough to simply tweet a hashtag. This is what most people will identify as Twitter spam. You should always write your tweet first and only add hashtags if it will add something to the tweet. Never write your content around a hashtag.

Hashtags are a tool that can be used to help bring more attention to your business. Hashtags allow users to find tweets on the subject they are looking for, and also allows them to find interesting information. When you use tags in your marketing strategy it is important that you follow these unwritten rules in order to get the most out of hashtags. The most important rule is to not put too many tags into one tweet.

The Different Types of Tweets

At their most basic level, tweets are messages that are meant to pass on information to other Twitter users.

Whilst there is no straight forward way of categorising tweets, you can group them in terms of their impact, and also the way Twitter treats them.

The Mundane Tweet

What I call the mundane tweet is a type of tweet that literally focuses on the person sharing it. It can be about where they have been, their experiences of the moment and generally how they are faring. To most users, they are boring and they do not add any value to the user or any meaningful discussion.

Mentions

These are tweets that have @ before the individual's Twitter handle. The recipient will, as a rule, receive an email or SMS notification. They will also receive the tweet in a 'mentions feed' rather than the home feed. There are three types of mentions.

- A 'reply' must start with @ as the first character. It is seen in the home feed of users who are followers of both sender and recipient.
- A 'true reply' is sent when the sender uses the reply button. In such cases, the recipient is made aware on which tweet they are receiving the reply.
- Finally, a 'broadcast tweet' is when @ is included but is not the first character. This final type of tweet can also be achieved by placing a period at the beginning of the tweet, such as .@lewisallanlove, which can be useful if you want to enable all of your followers to see a certain

conversation; for example, to announce a competition winner.

Retweets

These tweets are simply forwarded messages or links to relevant content from another tweet. They often come with 'RT' before the message. Links may be included. There are two types of retweets. A 'true retweet' is when you use the retweet button. On the other hand, 'quote retweet' or 'modified retweet' is when the original content has been edited.

Direct Messages

This is a private message that is sent between people who follow one another. It will not be seen by others and neither will it appear in search engine results. Such a message cannot be used for marketing purposes unless it is specifically intended as a personal answer by a customer care representative.

Promoted Tweets

These are ordinary tweets which can be replied to or retweeted. Nevertheless, they are paid advertisements. They can be seen on search results and are clearly marked as other advertisements are. They are highly favoured because they can be seen by a higher number of Twitter users.

Expanded Tweets

This is a feature of Twitter that shows extended content for certain media partners. On content sent from these associates, you can click and directly access pictures, links to songs and YouTube videos.

Broadcast Tweet

If you send a tweet to your follower with the @ symbol, this is a mention, and the recipient gets the tweet in their mention feed. If @ is not the first character, the recipient's followers will receive the tweet in their home feed. As previously mentioned, for these types of tweets, some people find it more convenient to use a dot (.) in front of @. These can be nagging to users if too many are sent too soon. For marketing purposes, it is always advisable to schedule their posting to certain intervals.

Question Tweet

This kind of tweet has the capability of sparking off conversation in an unimaginable manner. The person asking the question may simply be intending to start a discussion, or they may want to get a genuine, first-hand account about a certain issue. Questions which are catchy may attract a lot of attention. For example, if a question is about 'how to?' everyone will like to prove that they know something about the subject. There are individuals that will do anything to get to any questions and provide an answer to them. However, getting an answer is not always automatic.

Quote

This is yet another way of starting dialogue. What you can do is take a quote from a book, song, the media, or a movie and post it. When followers have started retweeting, commenting and some even criticising, the discussion is underway.

Information Tweet

This is a way of conveying important news to your followers. Some events have demonstrated that tweets can, at times, spread news better than the electronic media. Good examples include the death of Michel Jackson and the terror attacks in India. One drawback of these tweets is that some people are skeptical about them because they may be untrue. Some less savoury individuals have, in the past, posted malicious information that people have later realised was nothing but sheer wickedness. Not very nice.

Blog post Tweet

This is a strategy where a user exploits their Twitter account to publish their blog posts. If such blog posts are for the promotion of certain products or services, this can be a helpful marketing tool, although we'll go over this in a bit more detail further on. The problem arises if a user has nothing else to share and is always about blog post tweets. Their followers might get bored and start to un-follow.

Giveaway

This kind of tweet is applied where there are contests or promotions. It can be retweeted to numerous other users and has the capability of greatly increasing your followers. The strategy works best if there is free stuff, discounts or extra free stuff with each purchase. Caution should be taken to ensure that there is a free element to the offer. If it seems to be deceiving, your credibility could suffer greatly.

Spammer

These tweets can take two shapes. There are those that overly promote their marketing interests and there are those that are simply a nag. In this category, you will get messages about how to 'get-rich-quick' and miracle cures for acne. You can also bundle into this category the tweets you may see from people offering you '1,000 Twitter Followers'. More on why that particular offer is a terrible idea later. On the whole then, these messages perform poorly as most users will eventually block you. Not ideal.

All in all, the way you treat tweets depends largely on what you use Twitter for. As a marketing tool, you need to be really careful not to make your customers feel as if they are being treated as a mere 'follower' or someone to be sold at. For best results, don't jump into the habit of promoting your products or services until people trust you. It is also advisable to mix your promotional tweets with informative and sometimes amusing ones. As I've previously mentioned, and will continue to mention throughout the book, as it is the single best piece of advice you could take: only let 20% of your tweets be promotional. That includes tweeting about a latest blog post. Spend the remainder of the time promoting other peoples' content, engaging with your followers and talking about relevant news. If you understand how Twitter works, have a keen eye on how users react to different content, and are not overly promotional, you will see some great returns in using these different types of tweets.

Using Twitter In Your Online Business Strategy

Networking 2.0

Networking on Twitter is a great way to make yourself visible to your market and to make a name for yourself inside your niche. This could provide leads, references and many other opportunities. This is also a good way to engage with people who may prove to be useful: both other businesses and companies, and your own potential clients. Essentially, networking on Twitter is about identifying your desired social circle and establishing relations with members of your circle through communication; very similar in fact to real world networking.

It's important to identify people both inside your niche and outside of it you wish to connect with. You will probably want to connect with the major players - influencers - but don't forget about all the other people you may wish to become part of your social circle. Start with major influencers in your niche and work your way from there. Finding influencers is usually easier than identifying smaller players, so be ready for some trial and error until you find the best people you wish to connect with.

By having a well-developed profile and focused Twitter feed, it makes it easy for potential followers and people inside your circle to understand who you are and what you're interested in. It's important to be consistent with your Twitter messages and interests to attract the people who are truly interested in what you have to say. These are people you want to communicate with and include in your network. To build an effective network, you need to communicate. It means connecting with people and engaging in conversations. It may seem basic, but this is an often overlooked aspect of Twitter. In essence, it's a social network, so you need to socialise. Never forget about one simple fact: people on Twitter are people, even if they use a brand/company account. The main way to build your network is to communicate with those inside your desired social circle.

Creative and engaging hashtags can also help you connect with people inside your social circle. Even if you don't make it a trending topic, you will unite your circle with a personalised hashtag. Hashtags will make it easier for people to find you and your topic of interest. This is a great way to unite your network.

Whilst we have already covered the concept of balancing your tweet content, it's worth reiterating the fact that your feed should be a combination of core messages, retweets and actual conversation. This is the only way to build a well-balanced feed and to prove yourself as someone who is ready to socialise.

Ultimately, Twitter is all about communication, so you

should actively communicate with those inside your social circle. There are a number of ways to do this, but helping others is one of my favourites. It increases your social circle and makes people notice you. This is a great way to show your expertise and prove to people that you are worth following. Answering questions, offering helpful tips and sharing little niche secrets will help you build your social circle because people will know they can count on you.

One of the most effective ways to connect to people is to ask for help about specific topics of your interest. People like to be needed and many Twitter users are ready to provide answers and help those who seek assistance. This is a great way to connect with people and start conversations.

Retweeting is a good way to connect with people inside your circle. It shows that you are reading and appreciating their content and that you wish to share it with your followers. However, don't forget about your audience: choose truly valuable RT content to share. Never use a retweet to simply flatter someone; make sure their tweet is worthy of a RT.

Don't forget to thank others. Recommend them to your followers. You should be ready to present people inside your social circle to your followers. One of the most popular ways to do it is through the #followfriday or #ff hashtags, but it's not the only time that you should remember others inside your network.

Whilst the following two points don't really count as conversation, they can be very effective. Use them sparingly for the best effect:

Share breaking news

Twitter provides a very effective way to share all sorts of news. Do your best to stay relevant to your niche and offer news your followers and potential followers will be interested in. Make sure the news you choose is worth sharing. Don't focus too much on your own company or products: share general news in your niche and you can become your followers' main source of information.

Interesting tidbits

Fascinating facts, inspirational quotes, statistics and other interesting tidbits may be a good way to attract attention. However, you need to use them sparingly. Twitter is essentially about communication, so don't fill your feed with quotes and facts. A better way to share an interesting tidbit is to include it with your unique commentary or to invite people to comment on it.

Remember to not focus on the follower numbers. Followers are important, but the network you build and real relationships are more important than numbers. Focus on reaching people and building strong connections. The goal is to engage your audience and interact with people in your circle. That is more important than numbers. Also, don't follow back automatically. It may seem like a common courtesy, but it will only make your stream cluttered. Following everybody makes it difficult to find valuable information. This is why identifying your desired social circle is very important. That being said, you never know where a simple 'follow' could take you.

Never confuse spamming and promotion for real conversation. It is ok to mention your products and services from time to time, especially if you have a special offer or something exciting you wish to present. However, you should avoid making your tweets overly promotional. Never spam people with messages about your company and avoid talking about your products all the time.

Influencers and other major players in all the niches are those who often set trends on Twitter. These people are great examples of successful networking. Here are some examples of businesses and companies that are great at networking:

- Starbucks (@starbucks): This company engages with their customers and people in their circle on different levels. They also have specialised regional accounts.

- CNN (@cnn): They take networking seriously. It's interesting to note they made headlines in 2009, when Ashton Kutcher challenged them to a race for one million followers. Kutcher won, but it was a great way for CNN to present itself as a company worth following.

- Coca-Cola (@CocaCola): The company shares varied content and encourages people to post and retweet messages to increase the level of Twitter communication.

- The New York Times (@nytimes): They effectively use Twitter to stay relevant in the digital age, when less and less people are interested in newspapers. Editors, reporters and writers share personal tweets and encourage discussion.

- NASA (@NASA): This is a great example of a

specialised niche account that is both interesting and informative for the general public. They often launch specialised accounts for their missions, like they did for Mars Phoenix Lander (@marsphoenix).

Marketing Products on Twitter

Twitter can be a very effective tool for product promotion. However, you need to know how to use it wisely. It's all too easy to schedule a tweet about every product in your online store, but with Twitter marketing, balance and tact are probably the most important skills you need to master. Aggressive advertising and blatant promotion just don't work: people will simply un-follow you and never go back. If all you tweet about is your products and their features, your Twitter feed will have no social value to readers and you will never be able to turn them into customers.

For these reasons, it's important not to force advertising but to focus on a different type of content: advice in your area of expertise, useful tips, helpful information, and more. This doesn't mean you should never tweet about your products or invite people to check out your newest offer; after all, your followers know you have a business to promote. An occasional sales pitch or open advertising is permitted and effective. However, the majority of your tweets should be informative and engaging. Never shy away from communicating with people on Twitter and responding to their messages.

I feel like I am beginning to repeat myself, but I can't stress how important an informative, professional Twitter profile is. When it comes to promotional accounts, it really is a must-have. If you want to be taken seriously, you need to look and act professionally. Your profile should reflect this and it should present your business in the best possible light. Have a professional photo of yourself or your company's logo. Include a link to your website. Use the official company colours. Write an engaging profile and your followers will take you seriously.

Your Twitter messages should also be engaging and informative. Instead of spamming people with your products, you have to offer something to your followers. Never force your ads on your followers. Instead, offer helpful information before you try to sell something to them. This info can be as general as something related to your field, or more specific, such as offering advice on how to use one of your products. Whatever you do, try to be helpful. Followers want useful information and they want you to help them with their needs. If you fail to do this, they will turn to someone else. On the other hand, if you manage to provide helpful information and engaging content, followers will have more reasons to stay. Then, and only then, you can post an ad or use a more direct marketing approach.

Never forget about this simple fact: Twitter is a social media platform. In order to make the most of it, you need to engage in conversation with others. Even the best profile, interesting information and smart promotional strategies will fail if you never talk to your followers and other people on Twitter. To be successful on Twitter, you should talk to people: never give the impression that all you're interested in is talking to yourself. Retweet interesting content. Answer questions and ask new ones.

Talk to people. This is the easiest way to get your profile noticed. Build an open communication with your followers and they will be more ready to hear about your new products and offers. If you build strong communication, you will automatically make your followers more interested in your products and services.

Coupons may be a good way to offer discounts, daily deals and bargains. Coupons, if used correctly, can impact the effectiveness of your marketing strategy. Special offers, daily deals and coupons attract visitors. They make them more eager to check out your product page or your website. Make your coupons Twitter-specific to increase the awareness of your brand and your Twitter page. However it's important to use coupons sparingly or else it may stop being profitable for your business. Also, offering coupons and special deals for most of your products may, in some cases, decrease their perceived value with customers. For these reasons, you should carefully target 2-3 products you wish to advertise in this way. Make sure the coupons and deals are attractive to customers: always stay relevant and offer at least 20% off.

What NOT to do

Here are some things you should never do in your product promotion on Twitter. These strategies will make you look unprofessional and a little bit desperate. If this is you now, don't worry too much, Twitter is a forgiving platform. Instead, read over them carefully and be sure not to make the same mistake again. I'll just repeat it once more; the following strategies are counterproductive and *should not* be used for Twitter promotion.

Spamming

We've already covered what a 'spam' tweet is, but it's worth noting that there is a huge difference between posting regularly and spamming. Posting too often and using generic messages will get you nowhere. Especially if these messages are blatant advertising in the form of: 'click here to buy my product'. This isn't the sort of behaviour you wish to practice on Twitter. It's too aggressive, too promotional and too selfish. It doesn't take your visitor's needs and interests into consideration.

Promotional DM

Automated, promotional direct messages are a very bad way to build a relationship with your followers. These messages are made in the form of ads: 'click here to buy my latest book', 'check this link to see my Facebook page', etc. This is a bad way to communicate with your followers and it's rarely, if ever, productive. It disturbs the trust between you and your followers: they followed your profile and now they are tricked into receiving your spam. These actions often result in an un-follow. The bottom line is, they are not effective for generating sales OR building your reputation.

Lack of updates

Posting too often is something you wish to avoid at all costs, but infrequent posts are another bad strategy. If you only tweet when you want to post a promotional link and then disappear, you're sending the message that you are not interested in conversation and that you probably won't be there to reply if someone needs your help.

Lack of knowledge

In order to successfully promote your products and services, you need to be able to present them to your followers. It means you should know more about them than anybody else: you should know how a product works and how to use it. You need to have helpful tips ready and you need to inspire your followers about the many different ways in which they can use your product. If you fail to do so you will be unable to effectively present your product to your potential customers.

They are the biggest offenders, but ultimately, if your strategy lacks the social element and it doesn't engage with the person behind the tweet, chances are it's a pretty useless strategy too. Without wanting to dwell on negative points for too long, here are some more specific tips for promoting products or services, as well as special types of marketing strategies you may wish to employ.

Online Stores

You can use Twitter to effectively market your online store. The goal is to make potential customers aware of your ecommerce website and to boost your online sales. Instead of direct promotion, make sure to introduce your followers to your products and services in an easy, engaging way. Explain an interesting product feature or introduce a new product line. Talk about different payment options and shipping methods you offer.

Engage in conversations with potential customers. It's very important to stay active and reply quickly to any messages or questions. This goes for criticism and negative remarks, too. By not ignoring negative comments about your store and products, you are making people realise you care about their opinion and that you're doing your best to improve your online business.

Blogs and Websites

Promoting your blog on Twitter should go in two directions. First, you should present your content to your Twitter followers. Talk about your new blog posts and make sure to tweet whenever you write something new. Make sure the title is engaging. You may also wish to add a short quote from the post to make people click the link leading to your blog.

The second strategy is to focus on your field. What is the subject of your blog, what is your area of expertise? To have a successful blog, you need to present yourself as an expert in your field. Therefore, you should be able to discuss common issues and problems in your field. Engage in Twitter conversations, answer people's questions and offer expert advice. This is how you'll present yourself as knowledgeable in your field. This will make people more interested in your blog and its content when you advertise it on Twitter.

Using Twitter as a Customer Service Tool

Twitter provides a great platform for business promotion and direct interaction with potential customers, but it can also be used for customer service and support. Many successful companies, small businesses and professionals use Twitter to respond to their customers' problems and build effective customer service.

Some people believe it's impossible to offer a helpful reply in 140 characters or less, but the truth is that customers want to be acknowledged and offered help as soon as possible. A short, personalised reply with a link to a document or a more appropriate channel is often enough to help. It's important to act quickly and acknowledge a customer's needs.

There are many reasons why you should use Twitter for customer service. Most importantly, Twitter saves your customers' time. Phone customer service is very effective in many cases, but it can be very frustrating for the customers to wait on hold. Twitter gives them an opportunity to reach you quickly and easily. Additionally, this type of customer service saves *you* money and time. Twitter is a free network you can use to reach your customers. It can also be very convenient for your staff to respond to Twitter messages quickly, before moving to a new task.

Building a specialised account for customer service can do wonders for your company's image and reputation. If you offer quick replies from helpful staff, your Twitter history will reflect this. Even more, your satisfied customers will usually tweet about their experience or thank a staff member who helped them solve a problem. You can even turn negative comments into positive ones if your customer service team resolves an issue. Remember, those who hate one company will always be the biggest advocates of another.

In order to use Twitter effectively for customer service, you need to understand how it works. This goes for both technical aspects and the way people use this network. With a strict character limit and the fast nature of these messages, sending a quick and helpful reply is essential for effective Twitter customer support. It's vital that you send a quick reply to your customers. Twitter is a perfect tool for it. While 140 character limit may seem like an obstacle, a short, concise reply is enough to get your customers' (or a potential customer's) attention. Twitter makes communication immediate and reachable so it's perfect for customer support. This is why it's important to have knowledgeable people within your staff who will be there, monitoring messages & inquiries and responding as soon as they appear. If you are unable to help them straight away, it's still advisable to respond immediately, letting them know you've heard them and that you're working on the solution.

While you should be available to your customers, you don't have to wait for them to contact your company directly. Sometimes, offering the best customer support is about actively seeking what people on Twitter have to say about your niche. Offering a quick reply or advice to people who haven't contacted your company's account directly helps you build a good reputation for your business. It will also help you attract new customers and gain positive reviews.

On the subject of reviews, it's important to stay informed about what people have to say about your company. Make sure to monitor Twitter comments and customer opinions. This way, you will be able to track your reputation and what's being said about your business. Even more importantly, it gives you additional opportunities to interact with customers or prospective customers. Take your time to thank people who post positive comments about your brand, and you may even consider following your satisfied customers. However, be careful when offering gifts or discounts for those who post positive reviews. This may lead people to believe it's possible to buy positive reviews for your brand, and it's damaging for your reputation. Even more, the reviews will seem fake and dishonest.

At the same time, it's important to find negative comments about your company and interact with these unsatisfied customers. Ask them what the problem was and if there's anything you can do to make their experience with your company more positive. Try to make things better, and always apologise for a mistake. Don't be overly promotional in your attempts to win them over. Also, remember that a honest apology is more efficient than being defensive.

People like to feel there's a real human behind a reply. This is why many companies use staff pictures instead of a company logo for customer service Twitter accounts. Furthermore, you may even encourage your staff to respond via their personal Twitter account. Always add a signature to your tweets (full names work better than initials) to further personalise your Twitter messages. Customers tend to respond better when they feel there is an actual individual helping them solve their problems.

The best aspect of using Twitter for customer service is that customers can reach you quickly and you can respond immediately. However, Twitter is not a good tool for answering complex questions. It's also a very bad tool for resolving conflicts. That's why you should know when to direct a customer to another channel, such as email or your website customer support. This way, you will be able to move a conversation from Twitter to the more appropriate channel where a customer can get full support.

Just like with your normal tweets, it's important that you are not too promotional with your replies. The goal of using Twitter for customer service is communication, not advertising. Obviously, anything you do and all positive results will reflect in your company's success. However, using Twitter for customer service should not seem overly promotional or fake. Always respond respectfully and offer a reply to what's asked. Don't try to blind your customers with promotional quotes or overly promotional language. Customers need to believe that your support team truly listens to what they have to say.

Many companies and businesses use Twitter for customer service, and some of them even have separate Twitter accounts dedicated to customer support. This way, they are able to help their customers in the most effective way. Some good examples include Best Buy (@TwelpForce), which offers tech advice and customer support via this specialised account. Citibank (@AskCiti) offers customer support via Twitter. They list all of their team members on the official Twitter page as well as their working hours, highlighting the human element that's so important to customer service on Twitter. In addition to customer service, BT (@BTcare) lists links to their FAQ page and other channels. They also update their staff info regularly so their customers always know who's on duty at any given time. My bank, Halifax (@AskHalifaxBank), offers help with online banking enquiries and First Direct (@FirstDirectHelp) offers customer support 24/7. They also offer an email address that customers can use for contacting the company.

These are just a few examples of customer service accounts I've run into over the years, and whilst there are hundreds more which you could draw inspiration from, I think these accounts are nice examples of good practice to get you started.

Keeping Track of Your Twitter Success

So you may have decided how you wish to use Twitter by now. It might be for marketing your products, it might be for networking with the leaders within your industry, but whatever you choose to use the micro-blogging platform for, you'll need to be able to keep track of how you are getting on.

I'm going to jump right in and say it; follower count *does not count*. If you are using this as a metric, you've got it all wrong. It's an easy statistic to get caught up with, so if this is you, don't feel bad about it. Just make sure you use the rest of this section to pick out a more meaningful metric to measure.

When it comes to finding a decent metric to use to track your success, you need to find one (or multiple ones) that allows you to track customers generated through leads acquired by Twitter and/or track your Twitter reach. Whilst follower count could actually be used as a way to track your reach on Twitter, it's a metric that is too easy to manipulate, and once you taste the poison of spam tactics, it's all too easy to continue down that road.

My first suggestion of tracking leads can easily be measured through a tool such as Google Analytics. You may already have an Analytics account - if not, you can sign up for a free account with Google. Once you've signed up, logged in and hooked up your website to Analytics, you can quickly see how much traffic and customers are generated through your Twitter marketing. If you run an online store, you can also enable ecommerce tracking, allowing you to see where the customer came from, and how much they spent. Then you can really see if your Twitter marketing is working. Remember though, instant results are rare, so stick to your marketing plan (which we'll be covering in just a second) and keep going.

So when it comes to the second suggestion of Twitter reach, there are a few options to take. Firstly, and my personal recommendation, is clicks. It shows whether people actually care about your posts. You can implement link tracking through services such as bit.ly and Hootsuite. My personal preference is Hootsuite, as they also provide some good-looking reports than you can print out each month. By using these services, you can gain a valuable insight into how many people are actually clicking on individual links. The reason I favour this approach over retweets is that there is in fact little correlation between retweets and clicks. Believe it or not, many people will retweet a tweet without even clicking on that link. If you don't believe me, go and read Dan Zarrella's excellent work on the subject.

So there you have it, my two favoured ways to measure how successful a Twitter campaign is. The first measures actual return on investment, especially for ecommerce sites, whilst the second measures actual engagement. The headline figures of follower count, retweets, and favourites can all be used as metrics legitimately, but it's all too easy to manipulate such figures, and even when they're not manipulated, it rarely transfers into actual pennies in your pocket.

Creating your Twitter Marketing Strategy

So we've discussed the variety of ways you could use Twitter within your wider online business strategy, but how do we plan this? Social media marketing plans seem to be the holy grail for many small businesses. Spurred on by the pretentious preaching's of 'lifestyle coaches', it's easy to get suckered into the belief that there is a single PDF document that will answer all your questions, tell you what to tweet, and perhaps even do it for you. Then, this magical document will increase your sales overnight and you will be able to retire and 'live the good life'. Life doesn't work like that. With this in mind, here is my Twitter marketing plan blueprint. It will not answer all your questions or tell you what to tweet, and it will certainly not do it for you.

For me, a social media marketing plan is a document that outlines your strategy. It sounds simple, but many choose to complicate this simple definition by suggesting the inclusion of a timetable or other silly things. It's also worth remembering that your marketing plan will be different to your competitors, or to your friend's business's social strategy. To get started with your own Twitter plan, I suggest going back to those questions I posed at the beginning. Why Twitter? What do you want from it? This way, you can go into battle with a plan rather than blindly tweeting away. Tweeting without a plan like this won't get you very far. Instead, decide what you want, and how you will get it. Now, for the holy grail. On the following page, you will see a series of sentences, ready to be completed by, you guessed it, *you!* This will form the basis for your Twitter marketing plan. It's not a concrete formula, as things change, and you'll possibly want to add in a sentence here or there, but on the whole, this document will become your Twitter marketing plan. Tear it out (or copy it if you're reading it on the Kindle) and pin it up on your wall above your computer. I know you could just define everything in your head, but having it printed out in front of you in your line of sight makes it impossible to forget. Now, without further ado, drumroll please...

My Twitter Marketing Plan
I will use Twitter to...
I will achieve this by...
I will measure my success through...
I will review this marketing plan on...

That is it. It's not complicated, there are no hidden questions, just a simple set of statements that will be unique to you and will help you to set goals, measure them, and meet them on Twitter.

Where to Spend Money on Twitter Marketing

I'm a fan of staying lean and agile as a business. Reducing overheads is a good thing, so why have I included this section on splashing the cash? Well as much as I love trying to maximize growth and scalable ROI for as little investment as possible, I appreciate that sometimes you have to spend money to make money. It's not always an easy decision to make, and I'm not here to pressure you into one. If you're struggling to put food on the table, I wouldn't recommend investing in enterprise standard marketing tools, or even outsourcing the work. This book gives you all the guidance you need to really get your teeth into social media marketing, and if you get really stuck, you can always tweet or email me. If however you are in the slightly more fortunate position of having some money to invest in your social media marketing efforts, this section of the book will guide you through some of the available options.

Twitter Tools for Business

When using Twitter for business purposes it is wise to have various Twitter tools to help. These tools will help with various aspects of your Twitter business campaign.

Not using Twitter tools can actually be detrimental to your campaign as you will need to complete all the tasks these tools can do manually. Doing these tasks manually will be time consuming and you will not be able to get all the information these tools can offer.

Businesses should use Twitter tools not just to increase the pace at which they tweet, but also to keep control of their campaigns. Some tools are able to track hashtag usage, others help to find relevant Twitter users for you to follow. There are tools which can help queue your tweets to ensure that you are consistently sending out tweets even when you are not online. You can also see what other people are saying in your niche when you use these tools, as they track tweets with specific keywords. There are a lot of Twitter tools on the market, which makes research into each very important. I've picked out my favourites to run through here, but if I haven't mentioned the tool you're currently using, it doesn't mean it's not good.

Hootsuite

Hootsuite is a social media management tool which helps you to manage your Twitter account as well as measure your campaign success. It's the tool that I personally use to manage all of my accounts, plus any of my clients accounts I'm actively managing, rather than just providing advice on. Hootsuite can be used by any business from large corporations to the individual, as they offer a range of price plans and features. There are three price plans available, each targeted to a different type of user.

The price plan which would best suit the individual or

small business entrepreneur is the Free plan. This plan doesn't cost the user anything each month, but the features are significantly less than the other plans. The features include:

- Hootsuite conversations which allows you to connect internally with members of your team and other users in real time.
- Message scheduling allows you to draft messages you want to tweet, and set a time and date for when the tweet will be released.
- Unlimited apps allow you to manage more than just your Twitter account. Various apps like Instagram and YouTube can be managed using Hootsuite too. The free plan will allow you to manage five different social networks.

The next price plan is the pro level which is ideal for small to large businesses or individuals with a large social marketing campaign. The Pro plan will cost $9.99 each month, however it is possible to get a free 30 day trial first. The features in this plan include:

- Unlimited social profiles so you can connect to every single profile you have on any social platform.
- Google Analytics integration allows you to see your Google Analytics data on the Hootsuite dashboard.
- Facebook insights integration allows you to see who has been interacting with your Facebook page on the Hootsuite dashboard.

- One additional user can be added to your account which increases the number of team members you can have working on your social media management.

The last price plan available from Hootsuite is their Enterprise package. This is only for large businesses and you will need to request a demo before you can purchase it. The features in the Enterprise plan include:

- 5-500,000 Team members allow entire organisations to access the dashboard and manage the social media campaigns.
- Professional services will allow the organisation to customise the dashboard and receive customised training and simulations.
- Advanced security will protect company information and assist in the prevention of costly mistakes.
- Enhanced analytics will allow the corporation to access any report from a range of different analysis tools such as Google Analytics and Facebook insights.

Followerwonk

Followerwonk is a Twitter business tool which helps you to identify and grow your follower base. Remember we spoke about following the leaders in your field? Think you know them all? Think again. You may know many, but using a tool like Followerwonk will show you just how many other big players there are in your industry.

This tool is actually a side app from the SEOmoz company, but you don't need to have an account with them to use this tool. This tool can also be used by any business with a Twitter account, from solo entrepreneurs to large corporations.There are two price plans on Followerwonk, each designed with a different user group in mind.

The first plan you can get is the Free plan which you sign-up to simply by linking your Twitter account to the app. There are five main features which you can access with the Free plan:

- 'Search Twitter bios' allows you to connect with other Twitter users in your niche or within a target demographic.
- 'Analyse your followers and follows' allows you to see who is following you and who you are following to better understand your target market.
- 'Comparing Twitter users' allows you to compare how your Twitter campaign success is doing against your competition.
- 'Overlays of your social graphs' are a visual representation of your followers and the people you are following. You can overlay them to see where the intersections are and determine how that will affect your social media marketing.
- 50 results per page is the limit on how many items can be shown on reports.

The other plan which is available with this app is the Pro plan. The Pro plan is no longer a Followerwonk plan, rather a SEOmoz plan, so you will need to sign up with them. You can try the SEOmoz Pro plan for free for 30 days and after that time it will cost $99 per month. This puts it out of the price range of most individuals and is targeted more to the bigger businesses and consultants like myself. Some of the features in this plan will include:

- Rich engagement metrics allow you to see how other large Twitter accounts are engaging with their followers. You will be able to see data on retweets, @ contacts and tweets which have a URL.
- Downloading results into Excel makes it easier to analyse the data you receive from the site and allows you to manipulate the data to appear in the forms you want.
- In-app following and un-following saves you the time of having to go into Twitter to find profiles to follow or cut down your following list. You can do this on the dashboard of the site on this plan.
- Toggling between different Twitter accounts allows you to manage various niche accounts from one dashboard.

ManageFlitter

Being able to quickly and efficiently manage your Twitter account is the basis of ManageFlitter. With this site you will be able to grow your Twitter business, access various types of analytics and schedule posts for when you want them.

There are five different payment plans available through ManageFlitter. Aside from the basic account, each of the accounts will have the same features, which are:

- White list the Twitter users you do not want to follow.
- Copy the followers and following of a competitors account to quickly build up your account base.
- Search for relevant Twitter accounts to follow and connect with.
- Unlimited number of follows each day allows you to follow at least 100 people per day.
- Track the changes that have appeared on your account, from follows to people who are no longer following you.
- Graphs of the changes that happen over time give you a visual representation of what happened and when it happened.
- Schedule posts for the optimal times when your followers are most active on Twitter.
- Geo-target your tweets so they appear only in specific countries or locations.
- Filter your followers to see who the most important ones are and how you can connect with them.

The basic free account will only have basic un-following and search facilities. The other four price plans vary in the number of accounts you can link to on each of them.

- Budgie price plan will cost $12 per month and allows you to connect to one account.

- Parakeet price plan will cost $24 per month and you can connect from two to five accounts.
- Kookaburra price plan will cost $79 per month and you are able to connect from six to 20 accounts.
- Eagle is the last price plan and costs $189 per month, but allows you to connect from 21 to 50 accounts.

Each of these price plans are targeted to people depending on the number of Twitter accounts they have. Large businesses would be able to purchase the Budgie price plan if they only needed to manage one account. An individual with more than one Twitter account for their niche markets may need to take a higher priced plan which offers more account connections.

<u>Buffer</u>

Buffer is another one of my favourite tools. If you just can't get on with Hootsuite, I'd recommend using Buffer. It's is a social media management tool which focuses on not only Twitter, but also Facebook and LinkedIn. To make it easy for you, the team at Buffer have made it possible to sign-up for an account by signing in with your existing accounts on these social media sites. The main reason for using Buffer is that it allows you to add information to the site which it will then distribute it to your friends and followers throughout the day.

You can install a Buffer plug-in for your browser and there is even a mobile app you can use to share information while on the go. Buffer offers its users two plans, the 'Basic' plan and the 'Awesome' plan.

The free Basic plan and the Awesome plan both have similar features including:

- Analysis of your followers which includes who your followers are, when they started following you and when they are using Twitter.
- Sharing quotes and information directly from websites. If you want to share something interesting with your followers you simply highlight the text and Buffer will help you share it via Twitter.
- Keyboard shortcuts to the web application. There are certain shortcuts which will open the Buffer app while you are on a different website, allowing you to use the service without being on the Buffer website.
- Share images and videos directly from the website. You no longer have to worry about downloading and re-uploading as you can share images and videos from the website you find them on.

The Free and Awesome plan each allow you to use all of these features however the main difference is the number of posts you can manage and the number of social profiles you can manage. The Free plan allows you to manage one social profile per platform and you cannot add any additional team members.

The Awesome plan costs $10 per month and is targeted to organisations which have a larger social network campaign. You can manage an unlimited number of posts with this plan and you can manage up to 12 social profiles across the three social network platforms. You are also able to add an additional team member. This makes the plan ideal for any small business working with social media marketing.

TweetLevel

TweetLevel is a tool which allows you to analyse trends and activity levels on Twitter. You can see what influential Twitter users are saying, find out how influential you are and measure the amount of activity certain keywords and hashtags receive. The tool provides information which allows people to streamline their campaigns and identify which keywords and hashtags to target. You do not have to have an account with TweetLevel to use the service as it is completely web based and all features can be accessed from their website.

There are a few simple steps which you can go through to use TweetLevel in order to find out all the information you need about Twitter activity. On the homepage of the website there are two search areas, one for searching keywords and hashtags, and another for searching Twitter ID's.

When using the keyword search you will be provided with the following information. You will find out how many tweets have been posted in the last hour about this subject, as well as the last day, week and month. Graphs are also provided to show how many mentions there were over the last week. Other graphs will display the URL's which have been linked to this word and the Twitter users who have the highest influence.

When you use the Twitter ID search you will find the

following information about the user. You will be able to find out who they are following and who is following them. You can find Twitter users who post tweets which are similar to the user and who has been retweeting the user's posts. There is also a graph which represents the Twitter user's influence level. After a search you will be able to compare the Twitter user you searched for against another user.

If you want to find out further information about a topic or Twitter user there is an advanced search feature. Advanced search allows you to analyse topics on one keyword in tweets which only contain certain words or have been posted by a specific user. You can also analyse links with the advanced search or only look into tweets in a certain language.

Tweepi

Do you want a management tool which only works with Twitter? Tweepi is one of these tools which focuses solely on Twitter and does not integrate with other social media platforms. As such, it's really focused, and the team over at Tweepi are constantly developing their product around Twitter, and Twitter alone. Tweepi not only allows you to manage your Twitter account, it will also provide you with statistics needed to ensure your account is doing its best. There are three plans offered by Tweepi, although the free plan has very limited features. The free plan simply allows you to un-follow users, clean-up the list of people you follow and help find new, relevant people to follow. The free plan will also be subject to adverts while you are using the dashboard.

The first paid plan is the Silver plan and it is costs $7.49 per month. Some of the features include:

- Bulk adding of users to your lists, which saves time and effort. By competing this in bulk you will be able to add as many users as you want in a very short space of time.
- You will have access to the premium tools which allow you to allocate shortcuts, follow users via the Twitter search and sort the different areas of your dashboard through filters.
- The number of users you can see per page will be limited to 100. This allows you to view all the stats much faster, as you are not scrolling through many different pages.
- You do not have to worry about adverts as paid plans are not subject to adverts.
- You can sort and filter your information for all pages and not just the one you are on.

The second paid plan is the Platinum plan which costs $14.99 per month. You will have all the features that the Silver plan offers plus the following:

- You can view up to 200 items per page instead of 100.
- The follow and un-follow history column allows you to see when you followed a user and when you stopped following a user.
- There is no limit to the number of users you can follow or un-follow with this package.

- Klout scores will be loaded and you will be able to sort them. Klout scores will help you find the most influential people to follow, as well as finding out if you are following people who are not really influential.

Twitter business tools are important for anyone trying to use this social media platform in their marketing campaign. These tools will help you manage your account, find the Twitter users you should be following, see which keywords and hashtags are doing well and see if you are influential or not. By utilising these tools, any business, whether it is large or small, will be able to streamline their Twitter campaigns.

Buying Followers

Apparently, size matters. Social media doesn't escape this, and when it comes to follower size, people really seem to care. It's a quick metric that almost everybody can see, just like 'likes' on Facebook. As such, it's become a metric that businesses often use to weigh up the competition – to see what they're up against. The problem is, a follower count can easily be manipulated and there are an increasing number of ways to spend your money in order to do just this. It can seem rather tempting at first sight; '10,000 followers for £5' sounds great. Can you imagine the look on your competitors' faces when they next take a look at your follower count? Especially when we consider how difficult it can be to gain real followers 'properly'. The problem is, that the followers you gain aren't actually real. They're not being told by a 'Twitter master' to follow you, they're not even being incentivised through financial reward. What 'they' are – or more correctly it is – is in fact a piece of software. A piece of software that creates Twitter accounts, then follows a set person. I'll share some more details with you a bit later in this section of the book, some of which are rather amusing.

There are a whole host of ethical issues that we could consider as well, but instead of preaching moral standards, I thought this section would be better if I utilised a real life example. But, as a new media consultant by trade, I couldn't go buying followers, which I know is a bad thing to do, for one of my clients. That is one way to lose a client quickly! I needed somebody who I knew well enough to trust me in purchasing these followers for the sake of 'research', but also stupid enough to *trust me* to purchase followers for the sake of 'research'. I'd read about the dangers of purchasing followers before, which is why I had immediately ruled out suggesting it to any of my paying clients. I'd read it can really ruin a Twitter account if you're not careful, but if I was writing about it, I needed some first-hand experience. Finally, it struck me. I could just use my own account. I'm stupid enough to trust my own instincts. Perfect. What follows is my experience of buying followers, and why I wouldn't recommend it to anybody I actually liked or cared about.

I headed over to Fiverr.com, the online marketplace where everything costs – you guessed it – a fiver. Although it is better than that for me, as it's actually five dollars we are talking about. For me sitting on the other side of the Atlantic, it meant I was only going to get a bill of around £3.40 for my 'experiment'. Hunting around the site, it didn't take long to see a long list of offers; '400 followers and a tweet to my million followers', 'I'll send you 10,000 followers'. 'Get 25,000 followers to your account'. Each one was of course five dollars, so there was an immediate inclination to look for the 'gig' which offered the most followers. After thinking about it for a few moments though, I thought better, and instead opted for a gig that had some good feedback. Surely 2,000 people can't be wrong about gaining 2,500 followers overnight? Buy. I sent the seller my Twitter handle and sat back and waited. And waited. And waited. It wasn't until much later that my iPhone made a noise alerting me to a new follower, by which time I was in my local pub.[7] From then on, my memory blurs. Nothing to do with the beautiful beer that was flowing, rather the endless notifications coming through to my phone. By the end of the night, I had amassed an extra 1,000 followers (I think). This was far too easy.

The next morning, I logged on to Status People and saw the scale of the problem I now had.

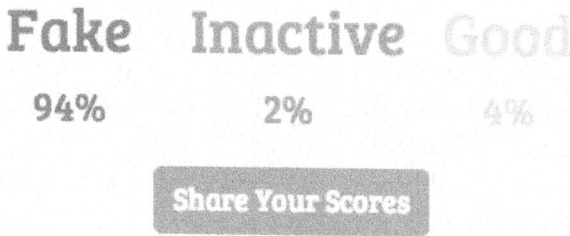

The seller had over delivered. By a lot. Whilst others

---

[7] The excellent New Zealand Arms, run by the Dancing Duck Brewery in Derby. May I suggest a pint of 'Abduction' if you find yourself frequenting.

were thanking her on Fiverr, I was cursing under my breath. I sat there sipping my coffee, deciding what would be best to do next. I actually thought about sending a tweet and asking for advice, but was put off by the thought that my message would only actually be read by 4% of my followers. It was really depressing. If you ever want to feel invisible, buy some followers. This point alone should put you off buying followers. If it doesn't, you'll probably find yourself very quickly going off the idea of tweeting at all, because once you realise that 94% of your followers don't even have eyes, it makes sending a tweet seem pointless. I did the only thing I could do, and began removing my followers. It was a long process, since Twitter only shows you a page of followers at a time. To make matters worse, I'd just recently published my first book, *Facebook Business Basics* and was getting real people following me fairly regularly too. The last thing I wanted to do was block a legitimate follower! I had to actually look at each follower's name and profile picture and work out if they were actually a real follower, or just a faker. After a while, I started to notice a few oddities, then I realised how the 'fakers' are made. The software scrapes the profiles of real people, copying their names, profile pictures and bios in order to create a fake profile. In order to avoid suspicion though, the software randomises each element and mixes them together. The result is that you find brand names following you with personal pictures. My personal favourite came in the form of 'Akilah Harvey':

Profile summary

Akilah Harvey
@AkilahHarvey1 FOLLOWS YOU

hey im hannah :) i love john ayer, one direction, justin bieber, the beatles, and Michael Jackson! im a dancer. love fashion. follow me! :)
xx
PA

3 TWEETS   **77** FOLLOWING   **5** FOLLOWERS   Follow

Akilah Harvey @AkilahHarvey1   5 Feb
ArtBasel About to take this exam...then it's off to Miami #ArtBasel here we come
Details

Akilah Harvey @AkilahHarvey1   2 Feb
The spirit of who we are can only flower into existence when we begin to feel the livingness in ALL things
Details

If you're after lots of followers like 'Akilah' (or Hannah?), buying followers is the perfect marketing strategy for you. Unfortunately, I've yet to meet a business owner who has described their ideal customer in such a way.

After quite a chuckle, I spent the afternoon sat with my phone blocking my fake followers. It was enough to send you mad. In the end, I decided that they'd have to stay until I found a better way. I headed back over to Status People to see how much of an impact my four hours of blocking had achieved. I almost cried when I saw the result. It was still 94%. The fakers were multiplying. That, or the Fiverr seller had thought I was worthy of some more. That was when I spotted Status People's latest offering; their faker remover tool. It took me all of three seconds to put my card details in. I headed straight into the dashboard and familiarised myself with the interface.

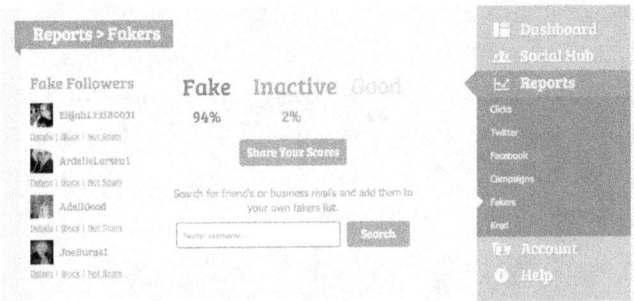

Whilst it wasn't perfect, it was infinitely better than blocking each faker directly on Twitter. All was going well, I was making a big dent in my 'fake figure' and I was beginning to feel like my real followers might actually start to reappear from the masses of fakers. Unfortunately, as software often does, it then just stopped working. I quickly sent the support desk an email and got a reply almost instantly.

"Hi Lewis,

If you press the find more fake followers button do any appear?

Let me know.

Cheers, Rob"

Impressive for a Sunday afternoon. The team at Status People is only small, much smaller than the likes of

Hootsuite, so I was impressed that they were proactive in sorting out a customer's issues. After a couple more emails back and forth I sent him this the following morning:

"Hi Rob,

Just tried again this morning, and it works for a couple of minutes, then just says 'Checking for new fake followers' and spins and spins and spins.

Reports > Fakers

Fake Followers

Checking For
New Fake
Followers

I really need to be able to block <u>all</u> of my fake followers. Any help would be much appreciated.

Lewis"

Again, almost instantly a response came back from Rob explaining how he was looking into my issue. He also mentioned that he was testing an auto removal tool, which if I'd like, he could test on my account. He would be testing a number of other users who asked for the feature, so if I wanted to be added to the list to let him know. The testing would begin in a few days. Not only was he looking into the problem (much more than most big companies ever seem to do), but he was offering to blast all my followers at once for me. Talk about going above and beyond. This was great news. I'd gone from being rather annoyed, almost depressed at the state I'd gotten my Twitter account in, to elated. Rob was my knight in shining armor, and he was arriving to slay all my fakers. He did warn me that I should be aware that it could take a few days for the system to start really denting my fake spam accounts but it was now going to start. A few days later my follower count dropped. Only by a hundred or so, but enough for me to realise Rob had kept to his word. Every day since, my Twitter follower count dropped by another hundred or so. I never thought I would be happy to write that.

Buying Twitter followers is a dangerous game. One that I played so you don't have to. Many people suggest buying a few 'likes' or some followers to get you started on social media. I would argue against that. When you gain 2,000 followers overnight, your real followers quickly get lost. If you've only got a handful in the first place, it becomes even harder to muster the energy to send a message. Instead, go and take a look at the section on 'Growing Your Twitter Following, Properly' again. I assure you, building a true following is the right way to go. You'll see more engagement with your followers and as such, more conversions. Social media is all about people, so let's not go bringing software robots into it.

Be Sociable

I've forgotten how many times I've said this in the book already, but it still amazes me how many businesses use Twitter as a marketing tool, forgetting that it is a social media platform, with the key word in the sentence being social. People join Twitter to be social, not to be sold at. The number one mistake small businesses (and big businesses) make on Twitter is 'broadcasting' their messages to followers, rather than interacting with them and providing them with relevant content on a continual basis. The main job on Twitter for your business is to interact and be sociable, not to sell. If your company isn't being authentic, or is just trying to sell directly to a follower, people will see straight through it and move onto someone else.

It's sometimes difficult to explain this in a way that is easily understandable, so I sometimes ask people to think of it in a 'real world' way.[8] Imagine you are chatting to your friends over a few drinks after work. You're sat in a

---

[8] This section was first published in Facebook Business Basics: The Jargon-Free Guide to Simple Facebook Success

trendy bar in the centre of the city and there is some music playing in the background. You're enjoying catching up with your friends from your school days, when one of the bar staff pops over and asks if you want to buy more drinks. You decline, saying that you're ok at the moment, but may want some more shortly. The bar staff leaves without any further conversation. Then, exactly one minute later, the same member of staff approaches you asking if you want some food. You explain you've already eaten and you don't want anything else. Again, they leave without saying anything else. They come back two minutes later wanting to know if you want another drink. Hang on - you told them only three minutes ago that you didn't want a drink, why would you want one now? Even writing this is starting to get me annoyed, so we'll stop here by unanimously drawing the conclusion that you wouldn't stay for another drink. In this analogy, the company's Twitter feed is the bar and you are the follower. Just like you'd leave the bar, and probably wouldn't return, you'd probably 'un-follow' the company, and have no intention of 're-following' at a later date.

You can see why it's important not to over-sell to your followers. But surely by not pushing the hard-sell, you won't see any gains? Well if we continue to use the bar analogy, how would you feel if, in the same situation, the bar staff were polite, courteous, even sociable? I've been in bars where the bar staff are happy to advise on drink or food choice, listen to my ramblings, join in conversations and even exchange jokes. Needless to say, these bars keep my custom. Now if you applied these principles to your Twitter feed, you'd be taking big leaps in the right direction to creating a great Twitter experience for your followers. Provide relevant and handy information - just like the best bar staff will tell me what wines go with what food. Chat to people about their social life, especially if it is related to your products or service industry. You could even go as far as to tell jokes. A joke a week might be gimmicky, but if you could relate it to your industry or products, even poking fun at yourself, you can really build your trustworthiness and authenticity on Twitter.

Many companies want to use social media to make more money, but by engaging with customers and providing an authentic, meaningful online experience, people will begin to feel a part of a community and be more inclined to spend with you at a later date. Twitter isn't somewhere to drive quick growth within businesses, but it can help you to organically grow your brand to an audience that cares and matters.

Be Consistent

To maximize your impact and success among visitors and followers, it's important to build a consistent presence on all social media platforms you intend to use. Having a consistent social media presence will help people remember you and your brand. Therefore, it's good to dedicate some time to make your social media profiles and content as consistent as possible.

Here are my handy tips for building a consistent social media presence:

Use Recognizable Visuals

Visuals are very important for building your identity on

social media. People remember images more than words, so make sure to leave your mark. Consistent images, logos, profile pictures and colour schemes are very important for establishing your unique presence on social media. Make sure you use the same (and easily recognisable) logo across all social media platforms. For individuals, a professional-looking photo is a must. Choose a clean picture for your profile and use it across all social media sites. Think about your brand colours and use them for your social media profiles and pages. Make people remember your unique visuals.

Establish a Consistent Communication Style

Having a specific brand voice is also important for consistency. Using a coherent communication style across social media platforms will make your brand more recognisable and unique. You don't have to try too hard, but it's important to stick to one writing style across the board. For example, don't be formal on one social media platform and conversational on another. Similarly, try not to send mixed signals on one social media site: stick to one writing style and try to maintain it for all of your posts. Obviously, the tone of a post will depend on the subject. There will always be times for a funnier post or a more serious, formal announcement. Still, try to find your unique brand voice and apply it to all social media sites.

Share Consistent Content

The debate is still on when it comes to sharing the same content across different social media sites.

Obviously, you want to share all of your important messages on all of the platforms, but it also means sharing repeated content to people who follow you on more than one site. It also means you won't be able to use each social media platform to its fullest. For these reasons, it's important to use a combination of unique and shared content for your various social media profiles. However, always go for consistency. Share a similar type of content. Don't neglect one platform in favour of the others, unless it's specific to your field. Even if you have more success on one social media site, don't neglect the others: remember to share consistent content on all the platforms.

Have a Clear Focus

To have a consistent social media presence, you need a clear focus on what you want to achieve and what type of content you want to share. It's important to have one common theme that visitors and followers can recognise. Presenting many different things all at once can be confusing. For these reasons, you need to think about the most important topics and issues you wish to cover and stick to them. This will make people understand what they can expect from you and it will help you present yourself as an expert in your field. Occasional off-topic posts are welcomed, but other than that, try to keep a clear focus.

Link Up all of Your Profiles

Don't forget to interlink your social media profiles. It goes without saying, but there are still so many business owners and professionals who don't do interlinking. It's bad for building a consistent social media presence. People should be able to find you easily on various social media platforms. Also, your profiles on different platforms should support each other. This way, you are strengthening your social media presence. Remember: you should make it easy for people to locate you across all social media platforms.

Know When to Break Your Routine

Don't be afraid to break your routine once in a while. Social media is not an exact science. People like small surprises from time to time. Occasional jokes or off-topic posts are usually welcomed, as long as you do it with style. Also, try to break your scheduling routine occasionally. Post an unexpected tweet or share some additional content on social media sites. Make people wonder what you'll do next. Remember: the goal is to be consistent, but not predictable.

You should understand that making a consistent social media presence takes time. You will make mistakes and learn from them. Recognise these mistakes and try to do better in the future. Also, don't forget about organisation and commitment. Use planners or the scheduling tools I mentioned previously for managing your social media content. This way, you will be able to manage your social media profiles effortlessly. It will also be easy for you to keep your social media presence consistent across different platforms.

Who to Follow Now?

Now that you have just about finished the section, may I suggest taking a proactive approach straight away. Hop onto Twitter and follow a few people. Firstly, me (@lewisallanlove). Why? Well I'd love to hear your experiences with this book. To me, it's a living document that I want to continually improve for others. Your feedback will help me do that. I also want to help you beyond the constraints of these pages. On Twitter, I can talk with you personally. So far, I've bleated on about Twitter and my passions, but I haven't heard a word about you. What is your business? What is your favourite food? Where are you from? I'm interested in all of these things. So, once you're on Twitter, follow me!

Next up are those industry leaders we were talking about. Forgotten about them already? Go back and read the section on 'Building your Twitter Following, Properly'. Find the important people and follow them. Then find out who they follow and follow them. That way, you'll have a pretty good feed of relevant industry news and you'll be able to offer something to your followers (when they arrive).

Finally, take a look at who is following your rivals. These are your potential customers. Remember not to get too aggressive with the marketing though, especially if they were someone else's followers first. All is fair in love and war, but we're in business here, so let's play nice.

4 GOOGLE+

Google+ doesn't sit by itself in the world of social media. There is Facebook, Twitter, Pinterest, LinkedIn, to name just the big players. So why bother with another social network? Why bother with Google?

Is it because Google+ links to your YouTube account? Is it because Google+ has Hangouts? Is it because search engine results are becoming influenced by social links? Well actually it's all of this as we'll come to see later on.

It's worth surveying what is out there and how Google's offering sits alongside the other options.

One of the biggest differences between Google+ and Facebook that I'd like to touch on at this point is that when you're logged into your Google account, anyone that's in your circles can recommend links on a Google search results page. If one of my friends have recently read and +1'd an article about the latest iPhone and I search for iPhone reviews, that article may well show up higher than others. That's not because the article is any better, or because it has more links, or because it's longer or because it's been optimised more efficiently, it's purely because my friend liked it. My friend +1'd it which means that I may be more prone to liking it. Of course, Google isn't stupid, if you repeatedly don't click on a link as recommended by one of your friends on Google+, it will reduce the frequency that it shows you such links. However, the more you click on links that have been +1'd by your friends, the more those friends will influence your search engine results page.

What Google have done is to bring social accreditation right into search engine results pages. Unlike Facebook, which works in a closed ecosystem, and Twitter which isn't that engrained to other platforms, Google+ is integrating its social aspect which is growing with its massive search presence.

A Brief History of Google

Google, the world's largest search engine (by a very, very long way) is possibly the most important privatised organisation in the world today. The modern world runs on the Internet – for something that is so new in real terms it is immensely difficult to imagine life without the Internet. And it's almost as difficult to imagine the Internet without Google. In August 2012, the engine went down for just 4 minutes and the entire world's Internet traffic dropped by 40%. That's the kind of influence the web giant has – and it's only getting larger as the company continues to grow.

This section will explore the history of Google from

the very beginning as a humble Ph.D. project right up to the giant that we all know and use today. This wouldn't be an easy section to write – a lot of research and fact-finding is needed. Fortunately, though, I've had a very special tool available to me. A tool that has in fact made the entire book possible. That tool, is the Google search engine.

The Early Days

Google started as a research Ph.D. project by Larry Page and Sergey Brin, both of whom are still very active within Google and together hold a 16% stake in Google's stock. Page and Brin are together number 13 and 14 on the Forbes 400 rich list, and first met at Stanford University, whilst they were both working in the computer science department. Page had begun to think about indexing web pages and Brin very shortly after joined him. Together they start working on their Ph.D. project that would eventually form Google.

Page and Brin's project, started in 1996, was originally known as BackRub, and was designed to find what websites link to a specific page. The rating of these "backlinks", as they're known, is still the fundamental pin in Google's searching algorithm, and is now called "PageRank", after Larry Page. Anybody hoping to get to grips with running an Internet business and generating web traffic will always have PageRank as one of their top considerations – it is immensely important to get on the good side of Google if you want good web traffic. The simple truth is that just *so much* web traffic moves directly through Google's web servers – it holds a majority stake in the entire world of Internet users.

After developing BackRub, Page and Brin moved on with their idea and what was just a Ph.D. project had started to gain momentum – the domain google.com was registered on September 15th, 1997. Shortly after this they both abandoned the Ph.D. side of things and took Google to the next level – working towards turning the engine (which had already been proven a hit at Stanford) into a viable business.

The company itself had humble beginnings in a friend's garage about a year later. It should be remembered that even at this time the Internet was still a very 'young' technology – Page and Brin were lucky enough to be working right on the edge of the wave that would very quickly become a huge and multi-faceted part of modern society.

The Growth Of Google

Between 1998 and 2003, the company grew enormously quickly and soon dwarfed all of its rivals. Google is a wonderful example of the classic 'American Dream' company – it offered a better system than all of its competitors, quickly grew a vast user base, and attracted enormous investment at the same time from a multitude of companies. By June 1999, the company had attracted investment totalling $25 million, on the condition that the Google founders would take on a CEO to run the company as the investors, Sequoia Capital, were not comfortable with such a huge investment going into a company without the formal business structure they were used to.

Eric Schmidt was the first hire as CEO in 2001, and it's

generally accepted that he, along with Page and Brin, steered Google in the right direction in business – allowing the company to grow responsibly and healthily. A difficult task bearing in mind the rate at which Google was gaining popularity among Internet users and advertisers alike.

A big change to Google's system came in 2000, when they started running text-based advertisements in their search results. This was the beginning of the monetisation of Google but at the start it didn't produce enough capital to support such a necessarily fast-growing business. As such, in 2003 Google announced a possible public offering of shares, and were shortly after approached by Microsoft to consider a merger. This deal never occurred (if it had, the technology landscape as we know it today would be enormously different) and Google went ahead with their IPO in 2004, raising $1.67 billion in capital, representing a market capitalisation of $23 billion. Within 7 years Page and Brin had built a company of the back of their Ph.D. project that could have bought the university it was started in!

The result of this enormous influx of capital and worth was simple – a huge proportion of Google's employees and other shareholders became millionaires overnight. Google – to put it simply – never had money troubles again, and was left to pursue other interests within the technology industry.

Further Growth and Expansion

Since 2004, Google has grown and grown into other areas, continued to adapt its search engine, and has been involved in an enormous amount of philanthropic activity.

By this time, the user base had grown to make Google by far the most favoured search engine on the internet, and readily available text-based ads generated enough income to facilitate re-investment into other commercial interests.

In 2006, Google bought out the entire Mountain View complex (which it had previously only leased a few buildings in) in California and this has become the company's centre of operations, home to the famous and secret 'Google X' labs and the head office, alongside some of Google's servers and a lot more besides. The company also started acquisitions of many other technology companies and encompassing them under the Google banner, including the prominent blog website Blogger in 2003 and – in an enormous deal – YouTube in 2006 for $1.65 billion.

Google's success, they claim, is in part due to their business model and maxim, put simply: "don't be evil". This is their unofficial slogan and was detailed in their 2004 manifesto:

"Don't be evil. We believe strongly that in the long term, we will be better served — as shareholders and in all other ways — by a company that does good things for the world even if we forgo some short term gains."

Google continued to grow up to the modern day, and has developed a host of new products and technology, such as the social networking site Google+, which, although failing to overtake Facebook, is still growing steadily as a social networking site. Other developments include the Google Drive system, which, along with GoogleDocs and Gmail, the company hopes will be used more and more in businesses and independent workers.

The company has worked – and is working on – a host of other projects and technologies. Google Earth was released in 2005 and has had huge success, beating its competitors hands down in true Google style. Microsoft and Apple – the two other technology giants in the western hemisphere – are the main competitors of Google but in many cases have been unable to get a foothold in Google's control of the market, particularly in web searching software – Microsoft's Bing engine has never lived up to the high hopes of its developers.

One of the largest 'fights' between the technology companies heated up in 2009. Known as the "Smartphone Wars", the struggle between Google, Apple and Microsoft to gain prominence in the mobile industry is still going on, though Google's Android system has again soared ahead of Apple's expensive iPhone and other competitors. The struggle broke out into a complex legal battle, with every company suing and countersuing every other company for various breaches of patents.

Google's web browser – Chrome – has also been a huge hit since being released in 2008, and was specifically designed to tie in with other Google products such as Gmail, Docs and Drive. In 2013 it held an estimated 39% share in user ship, making it the world's most widely used web browser.

Another topic of much interest to technology companies in the last few years has been Google's collaborations with various companies, including work with NASA in data-management systems and other subjects of mutual interest, including working towards an entrepreneurial space industry. Google has also announced partnerships with AOL, NewsCorp and Sky, and, most interestingly, has even signed a deal allowing The Pope to have his own channel on YouTube.

Don't Be Evil

Google's huge financial success has allowed its creators to follow through with their unofficial motto and start a philanthropic campaign. Both Page and Brin have announced on numerous occasions that they intend to help solve the world's problems with technology, and Google's financial status means it is more that capable of hiring the best people for the job at hand. Google's philanthropic wing, google.org, was started in 2005 with a grant of $1 billion, and has worked on various projects, including work into a high-functioning plug-in hybrid-electric vehicle. Other projects the charitable arm is focussing on is work towards renewable energy that can be cheaper that coal, and information-based charitable work such as Google Crisis Response (used to locate missing people and map a crisis situation) and Google Flu – used to track disease trends in the developing world.

Alongside philanthropic technological research, Google has continued to design products for its richer customers. The top-secret labs at Google X, although labelled by some as at least in part a popularity campaign, has started to churn out some interesting designs such as a self-driving car (Google has predicted that they will be available to the public in 5 years) and the impressive Google Glass – a wearable computer operated by voice recognition. These pet projects, along with many others, are expected to grow in popularity as the years go on.

Page and Brin are both private investors in a wide variety of philanthropic research towards "solving really big problems through technology". One that grabbed the world's imagination in 2013, for example, was a Dutch project to create a 'test-tube' hamburger. The project, backed anonymously by Brin until the results were out, was a success – and although it may be a long time till everybody catches onto the idea of a burger grown in a lab, the fact is these burgers *could* be made sustainably in the future.

Google enjoys its lab's top-secret and mysterious reputation, and cultivates it by not letting the public – or its competitors – know everything that's occurring behind closed doors. The same applies for a lot of Google's projects outside the lab, and this has worked in its favour – every new release from the company is followed by media attention and often studied obsessively by bloggers and technology reporters. Put simply, mystery has worked for Google.

The Future

The future of Google looks much like it's a past – a continual rise as a technology company with long-term interests and generally responsible behaviour. Google has not been without controversy over the years – they are being investigated for tax avoidance in the UK, and it has been involved in a fair few patent battles – but they look set to continue growing into new areas of the technology industry and develop their old systems.

There is a constant fear in modern society that some companies are too large to be sustainable and 'safe' for the consumer – Google has been accused many times of monopolising industries, and it is a truly vast company with 70 offices in 40 different countries. Even the word "google" has become a verb, meaning "to search something on the internet".

So, it is understandable that some people are concerned about the future when one private company is so influential in the modern world and looks set to be more so as time goes on. But if there is going to be a private company that has significant influence on the public, at least it's one who's motto is "don't be evil", is known for its charitable side, and works towards technological solutions to the world's problems. Putting it simply, things could be far worse.

What is Google+?

At its very simplest explanation, because I personally think Google+ can get a little complicated if you're not used to it, it's a really effective way to share content amongst the existing Google platforms, and it identifies contacts based on what you share, creating separate groups. It's a personal service, identify things for you, and you alone. That still sounds quite complicated doesn't it? Put simply, it's a lot more forward-thinking, and a lot more efficient than Facebook, with more scope for search integration, purely because it has the world's biggest search engine behind it.

Google+ is a social networking site launched by Google in 2011. Google+ allows you to build an extensive profile and share information with other people. It combines the features of several popular social media sites, such as Twitter and Facebook, to provide the best user experience. Another good thing about Google+ is that it allows you to protect your privacy and control who can see the information you share.

It has a variety of features, such as Circles, letting you organise your contacts into separate and bespoke groups, Stream, keeping you up to date on activities from your circles as above, Sparks, feeding you content based on your personal interests, and Hangouts, a group video chat app. These all help push Google+ in front of Facebook with its simple chat, and 'Like' functions. So that is the basic summary, but as this book is all about Google+, we'll now dive into a bit more detail.

Google+ Profiles

It's important to keep in mind that any Google+ account is based on a Google profile. Therefore, a working Google account is needed for Google+. The profiles were actually the first step into expanding user accounts on the network.

A profile connected to your Google+ page allows you to share certain bits of information with the world. You can share personal details such as your name, birthday, location or phone number. You can fully control which details are visible to the world, and you can always restrict certain bits of information if you choose so. A profile allows you to build a short personal bio, share selected info and add links to your web sites.

Also, Google doesn't require to share much information unless you want. You can build the whole profile using only your name and you will never be forced to share anything else.

The best thing about Google+ profile is that you can fully control the audience and restrict the information as you see fit. There will often be some info you might want to share with your friends but not your co-workers. Or something you want only your family to see. Google makes it easy to restrict this info to target audience quickly and easily. This is where Google Circles come in handy.

Google+ Circles

One of the greatest features is called "Circles". Google+ Circles is the feature, which allows users to create groups within their buddy lists. This feature helps the users to share the relevant information or content with the desired group of people. At the same time, it allows you to see the posts made by "Specific Circle" right away. Google+ uses a very effective concept of "circles". A circle is simply a collection of people with whom you wish to connect. Each Google+ account includes three pre-defined circles: friends, family and acquaintances. Of course, you may create your own, customized circles (such as co-workers, online friends, and more). You choose how to categorize people in a way that's the most convenient for you. Also, remember that you can put the same person into more than one circle, if you feel like this categorization works the best.

One important thing to note about Circles: putting someone in your circle means that you choose to follow this person. However, it doesn't necessarily mean that a person follows you back. Circles can work as a one-way relationship, so you can make separate circles for companies and other profiles you wish to follow but you don't expect them to follow back.

The best thing about Google+ Circles is that they allow you to share information with a specific group (circle) and not the others. This way, you can read the content from the selected groups and not the others.

You can assign a specific name to any circle. No one within a circle can see the name and other people within the circle. It works more like the "real life circles", the circles that are intangible and we all create in our minds. You can create various circles according to:

- Close Friends
- College Mates
- Co-Workers
- People we look up to
- Prospects/Customers

And so on…

It also works the other way around. You can always restrict the information you wish to share only with people in a certain circle and not with others. Sharing always comes with multiple levels of privacy, so you can customize these settings as much as you want.

For example, you may choose to share your address and phone number only with people in your family or friends circle. Using a handy interface and with only a few clicks, you can restrict this information (address and phone number) to everyone else. This way, you can protect your privacy while keeping an open and vivid Google+ profile.

Don't mix up Circles with Google Groups

I've seen some people saying that Circles is the newer version of Google Groups. I completely disagree, because Circles work very different than the Groups. There are three key features that make Circles way different than the Google Groups.

In Google Groups, all members know the name of that specific group:

- All members are aware of the purpose of group
- Everyone can see the other members within the group

It will be a more accurate comparison of circles, if you compare the circles with a "twitter private list" or the "Facebook friends list". Because people within a Circle is the compilation of people at your own end. That is why people within a list/circle have no idea about the name that you have given to the circle or the purpose of yours that why you made this circle.

If you want to share the post within the specific group of people/Circle. On the top right corner of the post, you will see a small tab called "limited". By clicking on that, you will be able to see the number of people who can see the post. You can even share the post with multiple circles or even with the combination of circles and individuals. Like I've mentioned earlier that you can control the visibility of your post to the specific circle. It is the great feature similar to other platforms like Face book , Twitter etc. For example, if you have a circle of prospects, you can share the blogs and latest happenings within your business with your prospect which is the concerned audience to that content. Similarly if you want to share a video of your pet with your friends, you can share it with the specific circle of your close friends while your prospects could not be able to see the post of that video. Even you can control that who can comment on the post.

You can arrange/re-arrange the order of your circles by simply "drag and drop". So if you want to see the posts on the top by your friends/family, simply drag the circle and drop it on the top and similar you can arrange the other circles.

Google+ works much like the other social networking platforms. But there are some great features which are available at Google+ and make it way different than other platforms. Google+ can help you out to think out of the box and create and integrate your marketing by going out and getting more audience. The feature of "Circles" can help you a lot to create the lists of prospects. So that you can reach out your audience to share you specific activities with them and can see their happenings as well.

Facebook vs Google+

There is an argument brewing. You might not be too aware of it, because you won't hear it on the street or in your every day working life, but online, this is a debate that rages.

Do you use Facebook, whether it be for business of pleasure? I'm guessing you do, because at last count the online community was hitting the 1 billion active users per month. Lofty heights, and that figure will only rise. I'm quite the Facebook addict if I'm honest. Most of my clients employ me for my Facebook marketing skills. I wrote my first ever book on Facebook marketing.

Do you use Twitter? The favourite go-to of celebs the world over, tweeting their opinions and rogue thoughts for fans to hear, follow and re-tweet. It's popularity speaks for itself, and again, the number of regular users grows and grows. I highlighted the real benefits in my previous book, *Twitter Business Basics,* so I won't repeat them all here. In brief, I'd say it's a great way to reach out to people you don't know, with a few hundred words' characters.

If we're saying these two social networking giants are the main big-hitters, then the raging online debate asks whether Google+ will take over the mantle and become the king of the social networking world.

Some say yes, some say no, some just don't know. For now, it's a matter of opinion, but there are several factors that mean that yes, it's quite the possibility.

After the last section, we're all up to speed with what Google is; basically the king of all search engines, and the one we all generally use when we're trying to find something. It is also a seriously money-spinning big business, built up from the very roots into the giant it is today. Google+ was launched in September 2011, and at first glance, nobody really thought much of it. When compared with Facebook's all singing, all dancing 'Like' button, and its ability to share, and in some cases, over-share, every detail of its users' lives, Google+ wasn't really much different, and it struggled because of it. However, fast forward a couple of years and with a few clever marketing ploys, Google+ had racked up user figures of around 300 million users monthly. That's a big jump, and it now threatens Facebook and Twitter's crowns on traffic and fancy apps alone.

Basically, Google is using its money and name to push ahead. Also, add in the fact that to use various other Google programmes, such as Gmail, you have to sign up for a Google+ account - a sneaky, yet effective way to gain users. Some find this a rather forceful tactic, but there's no denying that it works.

As for its name, Google has a lot of power in business, and companies and advertisers are quite happy to invest, whereas they're not so quick to throw money into Facebook, with previous advertising having not produced such amazing results for business.

Shrewd business use and a lot of research, based on watching how Facebook and Twitter have worked before it, means Google+ has picked up and righted the wrongs the former two made. This, twinned with the fact that the search element really comes to the fore with this new social networking giant, means Google+ has a lot going for it. Because of Facebook's ongoing dramas with privacy settings, it often means that posts don't appear in Google search results, however anything posted on Google+ will, which is an undeniable advantage in business, which is going more and more down the social networking route.

Should Facebook and Twitter be quaking in their cyber-boots? Whilst none of us can predict the future reliably, it's quite likely that Google as a business will push its social networking gem further into the fore, meaning Facebook and Twitter will need to up the ante if they're wanting to stay firmly on top.

Whilst Google+ does seem a little confusing to regular users of Facebook, there's no denying that it's a much more polished, efficient machine, and for promotional use, it could win hands down. Business will always win through in the end, as we know.

For now, the three major players in the social networking world can co-exist quite harmoniously, but one thing's for sure, the current big two shouldn't rest on their laurels if they want to stay top-dog. Based on how things are now, if things stay static with them, then Google+ will run through and pip them to the post.

Google are constantly trying to link their products together in a more efficient manner. You can see this through the linking of comments on YouTube videos and Google+ accounts. The reviews on Google+ local pages, also appear on Google Maps. And endorsements from Google+ pages are beginning to appear in search engine results pages.

What this means is for the small business who relies on Google so heavily to be found online, ignoring one of their products can be almost as damaging as ignoring all of them.

That's not to say that you need to be on YouTube, Google+ and embracing Google friendly search engine optimization. Especially around local. It does however mean that you need to be aware of how the products link together and why that matters to you and your business.

Ignoring it isn't really an option any more. Google aren't going to unlink their products. The links are only going to be embedded deeper and deeper. In the future you may see comments left on an article from a post on Google+ appearing in the search engine results pages. So when you search for "fence panels", you might see a review from your friend of "fence panels".

Google are already using Google+ profile pictures controversially in adverts. Data is what drives Google and if they can find another way to link two pieces of data together to enhance the user experience or increase revenue my guess is, they will.

Whilst their mantra is "Don't be evil" that mantra will only survive if they're making money.

I still remember the time when Google+ just launched and some of the social media "experts" believed that it is the "killer" of Facebook era. But nothing happened at all. Facebook still dominates the Social Media Platforms beyond reasonable doubt. So, there is no as such comparison we can make among Facebook and Google+. It is the reality that Facebook has about 55% domination upon all the social media platforms whereas Google+ has only 2%. That is why some people describe Google+ as a 'Ghost Town'. And when it comes to **consumer log in,** Facebook has about 62% login percentile. Whereas, Google+ has just 18%.

Interface Differences

Since the day of launch back in 2011, Google+ has been through many interfaces. There are number of changes on almost monthly basis Google indulge into their social media platform. When it comes to Facebook, the major change in interface was the conversion of Wall to Timeline. The colour of the interface is still the same though. Otherwise on quarterly basis, very minor changes are made by the development team. Since the day it started back in 2004, Facebook has changed and it is most certainly not the same as it was ten years ago. So there is quite balance in that comparison.

Profile & Chat

Google+ has more features to edit when it comes to building a profile than Facebook. You can edit individual tabs and a number of things on Google+. You can add the links to your websites and other profiles on Google+, whilst on Facebook, you can add your website only to your profile but you are not allowed to add the links to your other social media profiles. The chat facility at both Google+ and Facebook is pretty much same; you can add people to conversation, send and receive pictures and other multimedia through chat. But on Google+, there is something quite unique and different, which is known as Google+ Hangouts. Hangouts allows you to add up to 9 people in a conversation and can live broadcast yourself. You can even record a live broadcast session through it for viewing it later on.

Comparison Between Both Networks as Marketing Platforms

There are quite a few decent features and a very BIG audience on Facebook is available. And this is what any marketer/business needs right? The more people to reach out and the better way to market their services or product. Facebook pages, groups, profiles, video sharing facility, adding pictures along with the post, posting questions, creating polls, generating likes, sharing other links on Facebook (to your blogs or website), adding the cover photo which can represent your Business... it pretty much everything.

But when it comes to Google+, there are also some features which are very good. Like on Facebook, Google+ has profiles, pages, communities and other features but what makes it different and unique is the Hangouts, Authorship Markups on the profile to your website, circles, "what's hot", local places ratings. Google+ also has a decent audience.

Making Your Google+ Page Look Great

Making your page look good on Google+ is really quite important to a successful Google+ marketing campaign. It's your brand on one of the biggest social networks, so you really should be caring about it. If you're a plumber you wouldn't let your firm drive around in vans where your logos on a slant. If you're a cake decorator you wouldn't put and advert in the local yellow pages with a spelling mistake. It's these kind of things that you need to be checking, double checking and triple checking on Google+ because after all if your pages looks rubbish, it looks like you don't care. It looks like your brand doesn't care. Attention to detail therefore is paramount. Keeping it simple and basic like I've tried to throughout the book, what I'm going to do it go down the Google+ page and point out the areas you should be paying special attention to in order to make your page look great.

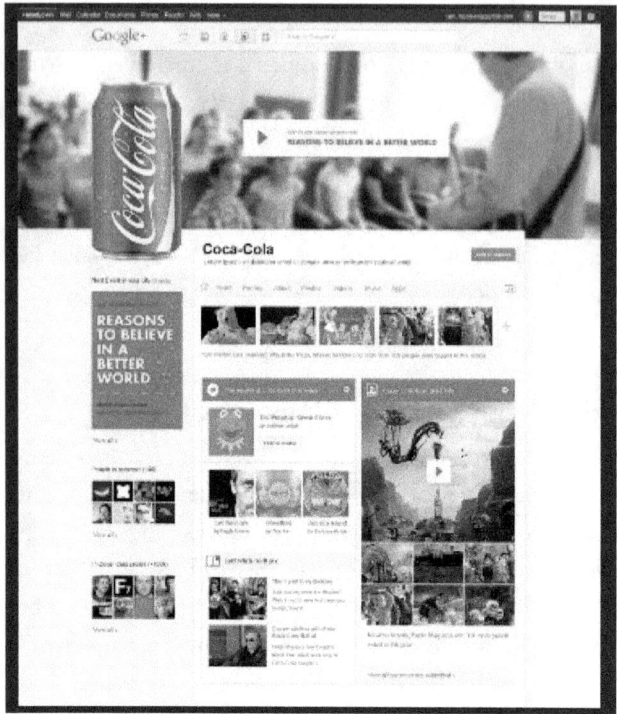

The first thing you'll see at the top of your Google+ page is a massive cover photo. This when you scroll all the way up takes up the whole screen on many computer displays. For me therefore this is really important to get right. You need to select an image or photo that represents your brand well and whilst there are some exceptions I believe that stock photos can never do that effectively. Invest in some decent photography of your shop, maybe of your staff, maybe of your work. Whilst this might cost a little bit in the short run, the long-term benefits of this I think are worth it. Imagine going back to the example of the plumber, his staff of ten stood outside the company offices with the sign written brands on either side polished and shiny looking. What does that say? This says this is a well-organised company that is professional, clean and tidy and aren't going to mess me about. It says this is a plumbing company that I want to deal with. What about a florist, or how about a picture of your shop on a busy Saturday afternoon. If you hire a half decent photographer he'll be able to give you some insights into nice angles and compositions; but imagine if you will that image of your shop on a busy Saturday afternoon with a really, really slow shutter speed with hundreds of people whizzing past it, and blurring the picture. Your shop stands proud against the backdrop of rushing shoppers. What does this say? To me it could say that your shop is a pillar amongst the local community, standing still and staying there whilst the rest of society moves by. You could also think more simply perhaps that this is a florist with a shop. It might sound obvious but there are many florists out there that don't have shops, they work from home and whilst there's nothing wrong with that if you do have a shop as a florist perhaps you'd want to sing about it. You want to say that you are a respected shop in your local area; you're not just operating out of a garage. It might be that photography isn't what you require, in which case I would strongly suggest hiring a graphic designer to give you an image that you can use for your cover image that is striking and looks great. The last thing you want is pixelated, poor quality images.

Moving down, though sticking with the graphic designer theme, you'll notice the profile picture. On Facebook, Twitter and LinkedIn these are all square but on Google+ its circular. This can cause some problems if you're just planning to take your profile picture from one of the other social networks and upload it to Google+. Quite often you'll cut off the corners of your logo. Again, this looks like you don't care. If you're not too confident in photo shop, get on that phone to the graphic designer again or maybe you've got a nephew or a niece who's a bit savvy with photo shop. You can always e-mail me as well. My e-mail address is at the end of the book and I'm always happy to help out my readers.

A little bit further down, you'll see a number of tabs and clicking on them brings up a number of different pieces of information:

- Your posts.
- Your images.
- Your information as a brand.

For me this section is really simple. You click the edit button and you fill in every box available to you. Social networks are pretty good at making their pages look great. All you need to do is fill in the blanks. There's nothing worse with a space where there should be a map. Make sure you input the details carefully and you'll be sure to have a great looking Google+ page in no time.

I've included a link to a cheat sheet at the end of the book and I've posted the graphic in as well. For me this is really handy to give to your designer, it gives them all the required information for image sizes and it helps you to visualise what your page will look like when you've filled it up. Getting the right image sizes from your graphic designer is really, really important because having distorted images, whether they're cropped wrong, pixelated or blurry just doesn't look good. Make sure you care enough about your brand to make it look as good as it does in the real world.

Enabling Authorship

Google Authorship is a feature which enables you to link your published content on any specific domain with your Google+ Profile. Note that Authorship will only work on a Google+ Profile at the time of writing, and not a page. However, you can enable Publisher rights instead. More on that later.

Google announced in 2013 that they now support authorship mark-up for Google+ which means authors can connect their content on Google+ from all around the internet.

Authorship is indeed a pretty awesome way to provide writers and authors more visibility during search results. And at the same time, it assigns a face to the one who is looking at results. It is a great way to market yourself and attract more clients if you are only relying on your website. Here is how it looks on a Google search results page:

Inside Google+ — How the Search Giant Plans to Go :
www.wired.com/epicenter/2011/06/inside-google-plus.../1

by Steven Levy · in 838,229 Google+ circles · More by S
Jun 28, 2011 – Follow **@stevenlevy**. **Google**, the world's
company, is formally making its pitch to become a major
networking.

So in order to set this up, you'll want to head over to the Authorship signup page (https://plus.google.com/authorship). You'll also need to make sure you have a profile photo with a recognisable headshot and make sure a by-line containing your name appears on each page of your content (for example, "By

Steven Levy"). Make sure your byline name matches the name on your Google+ profile. Don't go using fluffypony96 on your blog and Claire James on your Google+ profile. Finally, you'll need to verify you have an email address (such as stevenlevy@wired.com) on the same domain as your content. There is a way around that if you don't have an email address on the same domain, but I'll leave it to Google to explain that one.

Organize You Google+ Profile

Google use the image for your Authorship direct from your Google+ Profile. Which means you are required to create your own Google+ account. Of course, you should probably have one of those already by this point in the book.

Once you are done with creating your profile, you need to upload a photo to your profile image, which should look good in full size or even in thumbnail. After that fill out the information like the occupation you have, education and it will help people to recognize you.

After that, it is more important to add the complete URL and name of your Blog/Website. In the section called "Contributor to". Next step is to click the edit button then scroll down to the Contributor Section, and add the custom link and fill out the URL and label fields. Make sure, you are specifying the name of your homepage.

When you're done, just hit the Save button and then click on Done edit at the top of the page. Make sure by double checking the contributor section.

Configure rel="author" for Other Blogs

Once you are done with proper configuration for your Google+ profile, you need to set up rel="author" on single-author blogs.

You will be required to create a link to your Google+ Profile of yours if you have done work over other pages or blogs where your writer material is published. You need to creak a link which include rel="author" attribute to your Google+ Profile.

Google+ Publisher

Enabling Google+ Publisher status will allow your brand to sit in the Google Knowledge Graph (providing Google thinks you're worthy). Here's how it looks on Google:

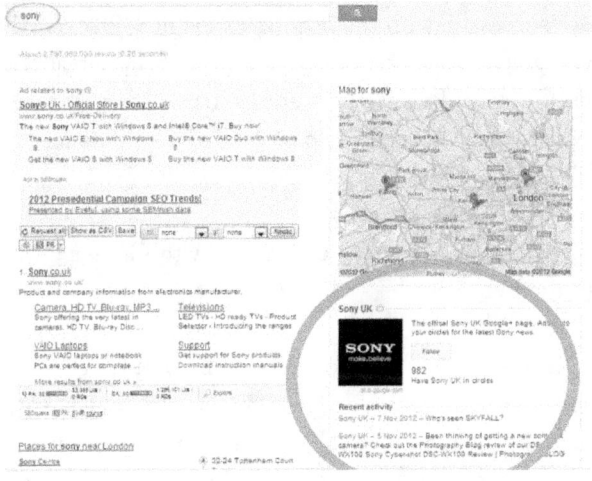

In order to connect this up, you'll need to add in a line of code or two. If you're uncomfortable doing this, just have a word with a competent web developer, or drop me an email. In short, here is the code you'll require:

```
    <a
href="https://plus.google.com/123456789123456789
rel="publisher">
```

Connecting Your YouTube Account

Google+ has a new strategy to make your social media presence consistent by having a single identity across all over your social media profiles. And that's the reason why they are testing some beta feature of linking your YouTube channel up with your Google+ Profile Page.

This is indeed a great news for those who have a very decent number of followers on their YouTube channel, and are looking forward to make their YouTube Channel more successful with the help of a Google+ Profile. At the same time, it is a great news for those who already have their Google+ Profile and want to market their services or products more with the help of a YouTube Channel.

Let's take a look how it actually works.

How to Link up YouTube Channel with Google+ by opt into the Beta Test

Make sure that any Google account you have is already associated with your YouTube channel and it has its own Google+ account as well. If you want to set up a new profile for Google+, then go to the website http://plus.google.com and follow the instructions to create a new profile.

If you already have a Google+ profile and want to

connect to your YouTube channel, all you need to do is add your Google account as an associated account with your YouTube channel as manager for the page.

Once you are done with setting up the Google+ and YouTube profiles, the next step is to connect your Google+ page (which is a BETA version as of writing). You will find it under advanced account settings.

Then select one of the three given options, and after you're done with that, you can tap into the Google+ community as BETA tester to share the experience of yours.

Advantages of Linking up Google+ with YouTube

You can have the access to many different features by connecting your Google+ profile with YouTube. You can add tools such as multiple managers for your channel, you can give a name or edit the existing name of your YouTube channel the same way as your brand page on Google+. Which means a greater flexibility. And you can even make that name consistent with your profile at Google+. The other perks you can have are like YouTube tab on your Page, you can easily broadcast from Hangouts the same stream of your YouTube plus seamless capabilities of video sharing.

The duration period of this BETA testing service is about 14 days. Which means that you have the choice to participate and can choose to unlink the both accounts of yours within that duration. If you do not unlink the account within that time, the changes will remain constant and it cannot be undone.

The facility or feature of cross linking within 2 different

social media tools is just a beginning of the whole change I feel Google will be implementing over forthcoming years. Why? Well having accounts linked allows you to market your business through the same account on different channels. Good for business. Good for the web.

You can also join the discussion upon this BETA service over Google+ Community and can even share the experience and the results with others who are looking or planning to integrate their YouTube channel with Google+.

Engaging On Google+

Engaging with your followers on Google+ is vital. I've previously stated that it's better to have 100 fans that are engaged, than 100,000 that aren't. This is certainly true on Google+.

What is the point of having thousands of fans who don't engage with you. They don't talk to you, they don't +1 any posts, they don't click on any links, they don't acknowledge any photos and they don't watch any of your videos. You're pushing content out into a black hole. Nobody is reading it and it's having no effect on your business. You need to engage your fans from the beginning as with any social media network. Facebook, Twitter, Google+, LinkedIn, they all revolve around engagement and enhancing your engagement should be the number one thing on your to-do-list. The following chapter goes over this concept in more detail, but remember to keep engagement at the front of your mind as we whizz through this chapter.

Creating a Strategy for your Google+ Campaign

This following section is lifted almost verbatim from the Twitter section. The reason for this is simple, it was well received and applies equally to Google+. So often I hear social media marketers, in fact marketers in general, over emphasizing campaign strategies when in reality, the best ones are usually the simple ones. Of course, you can add fairy dust over the top and dress the following up all you like, but my opinion is that a strategy should be kept simple and easy to follow. That way, you know when you're going off topic. Anyway, that's why I've decded to reuse this section. For those of you who have read my previous book, I'm sure you understand.

Social media marketing plans seem to be the holy grail for many small businesses. Spurred on by the pretentious preaching's of 'lifestyle coaches', it's easy to get suckered into the belief that there is a single PDF document that will answer all your questions, tell you what to tweet, and perhaps even do it for you. Then, this magical document will increase your sales overnight and you will be able to retire and 'live the good life'. Life doesn't work like that. With this in mind, here is my Google+ marketing plan blueprint. It will not answer all your questions or tell you what to tweet, and it will certainly not do it for you.

For me, a social media marketing plan is a document that outlines your strategy. It sounds simple, but many choose to complicate this simple definition by suggesting the inclusion of a timetable or other silly things. It's also worth remembering that your marketing plan will be different to your competitors, or to your friend's business's social strategy. To get started with your own Google+ plan, I suggest going back to those questions I posed at the beginning. Why Google+? What do you want from it? This way, you can go into battle with a plan rather than blindly posting away. Posting without a plan like this won't get you very far. Instead, decide what you want, and how you will get it. Now, for the holy grail. On the following page, you will see a series of sentences, ready to be completed by, you guessed it, *you!* This will form the basis for your Google+ marketing plan. It's not a concrete formula, as things change, and you'll possibly want to add in a sentence here or there, but on the whole, this document will become your Google+ marketing plan. Tear it out (or copy it if you're reading it on the Kindle) and pin it up on your wall above your computer. I know you could just define everything in your head, but having it printed out in front of you in your line of sight makes it impossible to forget. Now, without further ado, drumroll please…

My Google+ Marketing Plan
I will use Google+ to...
I will achieve this by...
I will measure my success through...
I will review this marketing plan on...

That is it. It's not complicated, there are no hidden questions, just a simple set of statements that will be unique to you and will help you to set goals, measure them, and meet them on Google+.

Driving Traffic to your Google+ Page

When it comes to driving traffic to your Google+ page, it can often be difficult to think where to start. It needn't be though; the best ways of driving the traffic to your Google+ page are always the simplest. If you send out emails to people put a link to your Google+ page in the signature. That way every time you send an email to somebody they see that you've got a Google+ page. You could maybe print it on your receipts that you give your customers or maybe you add it to your order confirmation that every customer receives when they place an order on your website. These are the obvious places to put it and this is what drives the most traffic, however it would be a bit unfair of me to just state that and say it's up to you because no doubt after a while you'll be wondering why isn't working. This is a common mistake small business owner's make. Placing a link to their social media accounts on emails and receipts and just expecting it to work. Unfortunately it's not quite that simple. Think of it as a call to action, you need to give the customer a reason to visit your page. I'm not necessarily talking about giving them 10% off when they circle you on Google+ or like you Facebook or follow you on Twitter. What I'm talking about is asking them a question, asking them to go onto their social media and engage with you. You've probably seen the signs on posters all across the country, on TV adverts and even on radio adverts saying like us on Facebook. The one word I'd say is, why? Why would the customer want to like you on Facebook or circle you on Google+? You haven't told them why they should. Give them a reason; ask them something. One of my favourite fish and chips shops near me got on their boxes- let us know what you thought on Facebook. They're not directly asking for a like but by god do they get some. They're asking the customer a question, they're asking them to directly engage with them and they're doing it in such a way that suggests that there might be a person at the other end of that computer who wants to know what there meal was like. When it comes to driving traffic to your Google+ page, you need to be thinking along the same lines. Sure, place links in prominent places such as email signatures, and yes, on the receipts or packaging that you use if you could get them printed so it says circle us on Google+, that's great. However, take it a step further and ask them to engage with you at that point. Make it sound like you're a human at the other end, after all you are. It's something so simple, but no one's doing it. Start now and you could really see the benefits later.

Using Google+ Hangouts

Are you looking to add some flashy video to your Social Media Marketing? With the help of Google+ Hangouts, you can make it happen relatively easily. By using Google+ Hangouts, you can perform multiple tasks at the same time e.g.:

- You can use the video chat with up to 9 people instantly.
- You can share files and documents.
- You can chat alongside while watching a video over YouTube together.
- You can share your screen with others.
- You can even record live chat session for viewing it later.
- You can even broadcast your live chat to anyone.

New to Google+ Hangouts?

Google+ Hangouts is simple and easy to use and, of course, is free. All you need to do is to create a Google+ account and then click the button says "Start Hangout". It's that simple. All you need to do is to click on the green button and then decide whom you want to invite.

Get Ready to Be Creative!

I have personally figured out four very basic and creative ways to use Hangouts for bringing in more business that I have utilised with clients.

1. Start Working by Collaborations (Crowdsourcing)

Google+ Hangouts is an ideal place where you can share the ideas of yours for new or existing products, services and even can offer solutions to you audience.
It is a place where you can provide valuable advice and expertise to your prospects. And because the content often spreads, it will help to convert the prospects into actual

customers.

2. Questions/Answer Sessions

Asking questions can help you out a lot in order to improve the quality of your services/product. You can collect very valuable information from your customers through Q/A sessions, which means it will help you to improve the experience of your customers and business as well.

3. Create A Workshop or Demonstration

One of the best and easiest way to give value to the customers while endorsing your business is to create a demonstration or workshop. It is the best practice for the businesses who are more viable at one-on-one demonstrations. Workshops can help you to convince your audience in order to convert them into actual customers. You can provide the audience with your contact information too and encourage their questions at a later date too. If you're in their phone as the person to call when they need advice on something, you're on to a winner! They'll be converting into a paying customer sooner rather than later!

4. More Giveaways, Meaning More Customers

It is the best practice, especially at the end of every year when your store room is stacked up with last season's products. It will drive a huge amount of traffic to your Google+ page which means enhanced exposure and perhaps a few more sales. People who will test your service or product will recognise the value of that product and become a customer. Of course, you need to engage your fans and make sure that you are providing your audience the product or service that can help them and not just a rubbish product at a discounted price.

Google+ Communities

One of the coolest feature of Google+ is Google+ Communities. It's indeed a great opportunity for the people who want to market their brand or product because Google+ Communities allows you to network, build and engage their businesses.

What is a Google+ Community?

It is a place to engage and meet the people who shares the same interest as you do. if you were facing any problems in engaging the audience in the past, then probably it's the best time to take a 'second look' over the topics and active communities that you might be interested in.
You can create communities which could be Public or Private, putting discussion over almost every possible topic to this is the right time to jump in and market yourself in a better way.

How a Google+ Community Can Benefit Your Business

In almost every single aspect you can think of, Google+ Community can benefit a business of yours. All you need to do is to consider some reasons for joining the

Communities at Google+

You can grow you network by the help of sharing your expertise and knowledge with the community who shares the same interest of yours. You can easily find the people who are passionate about the topic that matches yours. You can answer the questions by people and can share your thoughts.

With help of Google+ Communities, you can make a well focused group for the business of yours. So make sure while joining community/communities that you have to get some good impact for your business through listening to the discussion. If you got a question to ask, yes you should go ahead and ask the question, make your contribution in different discussions.

You can discover many new ideas through discussions for your blog articles or even get the better idea to make your services or the products of your business better.

You can start your own discussions as communities allow you to do so. it means that you can post an article or might share something that can grab the attention of your target audience.

You can even drive the traffic to your website by engaging the other people from the communities. As it is one of the best opportunity to post and article or probably for sharing some content from your website.

Tips & Thing That You Should Consider

Here are some tips (if you're going ahead) to find the communities that suites your Business:

- You can search or reach your target market with

the help of Searching them by Topics.
- You can even use the Keywords which are useful for your business.
- With the help of searching the competitors of your business.

If you want to start your own Google+ Community it's even better. It's really easy and take less than 5 minutes but make sure one thing, you are going to put some useful content in the community. Though it takes some time to seed anything with beneficial content. But after some time, you will definitely get there.

- First of all, add few lines in the About section.
- Then assign by going into the tab of settings, your can add multiple owners and moderators.
- You can add different topics which can be seen right in the side bar, then seed these topics with quality content.
- You can even made some rules for your community.
- Then you can even edit the Privacy if your don't want to make it a Public Community.

In conclusion, the reason why you should embrace Google+ Communities is just to make your marketing strategy more viable and to reach a wider audience and connect people and make them believe that YOU hold the key to their solutions. Of course, you do actually need to spread that answer, holding without sharing isn't very nice now, is it?

Google Advertising

Advertising is the one word that scares all small business owners it seems. The more I talk to people, the more I realize that they're scared of advertising, especially online. They either think it's going to cost thousands of pounds or it won't produce any results. Of course that is possible. You can spend thousands of pounds on advertising and yes, if done badly it might not produce results. However, done well, advertising online can be extremely lucrative.

I'm going to keep this section short and sweet, as advertising within Google+ hasn't really began yet in the same way it has on Facebook. Rest assured, I'll be keeping my eye out though, and as and when I deem necessary, there will be an updated version of this book available!

AdWords is perhaps the most well-known online advertising platform. It allows you to place adverts on the Google search networks. Predominately this means that you appear for certain key words on Google. You pay a small price, normally pence or cents to appear for certain key words that you define. You only pay when your link is clicked.

What this means is that you're only paying for qualified leads that are actively searching for your product or service.

If you're a plumber, based in Manchester, one of your key words could be "plumbers in Manchester". You could bid 50p for that key word and if someone was to search and click on your link you would pay Google 50p. However, that person then might convert into a paying customer who might pay £50.00 for a boiler service or

£2,000.00 for a bathroom refit.

For some industries, Google AdWords works better than others and as such the cost per click (or CPC) goes up. For other industries, it is not so lucrative or perhaps the profit margins aren't as great so the cost per click comes down.

For some reason though, despite knowing this, some small business owners are still scared silly by the thought of spending money on advertising.

One of my clients (we'll call her Sarah), was particularly worried about this. However, when I looked at her business a bit further I saw she was spending money on flyers. The flyers were costing her around about 6 pence for each one. We worked out that half of them would end up on the floor so really it was costing her 12 pence for a flyer to go home with someone. The person then would have to go onto their computer and type in Sarah's web address.

5 PINTEREST

Why Pinterest? Well, Pinterest is a social media network that is very different form the others out there. Whilst you can share pictures on Facebook and Twitter and even Google+, Pinterest is all about images. It's a visual social network, and as such it's developed a bit of a cult following. People love browsing through Pinterest boards for inspiration for there new lounge, or even looking at recipes for dinner that night and because of this Pinterest users are a lot more open to businesses in my opinion, whereas Facebook and Twitter users are there to interact with their friends. Pinterest users are looking for inspiration, and really if that inspiration comes from a friend or a company, providing it delivers, i.e. it inspires them; the user doesn't really mind. What this means is that Pinterest is a bit of a gold mine for marketing your business. It's very different from Facebook, Twitter, Google+ and LinkedIn, so it would be juvenile of me to suggest that it's better than all of them. It's different, but it's also incredible and what's better is just like it's fun for it's users to use, Pinterest is incredibly fun to use as a marketer or an entrepreneur. It's a tool that will feel less like work and more like play.

Pinterest isn't a marketing channel that sits alone or at least it shouldn't. I'm a firm believer that no single marketing channel will ever produce significant results without significant luck. By that I mean, if you put all your eggs into one basket, whether that is Pinterest, print advertising or even television advertising. The chances of it actually succeeding in the modern world where everything's multi-channelled and brands need to be everywhere all the time; being just on one channel probably won't work. That's not to say you need to be on every social media network, on every TV station, on every radio station, in every magazine and newspaper. However, if you look at the most successful brands, nine times out of ten they are in fact on all those channels. But, for a small business where television is usually out of the question, print is often too expensive, along with radio. What should you take from this? Well, you're probably already on more than one channel. By that I mean, if you have a shop, you've got a window. That is a marketing channel. You might do some work with the local magazine or newspaper, that's another channel. If you're now looking at Pinterest, that would be another. If you've got a website, that's a channel. Just because it's yours and you own in, doesn't mean it's not a marketing channel. Bearing this in mind, this chapter will look at how Pinterest sits within a wider marketing strategy. We've acknowledged the fact that Pinterest cannot be your only marketing strategy. Instead, it should sit inside either an existing one, or a new strategy that you will be using in your business going forward.

A Brief History Of Pinterest

Pinterest is the classic 'small, strong start up' story in this information age. The company has grown from strength to strength since it was founded in 2009 by Ben Silbermann – a former Google employee – in a small apartment somewhere in New York. The start-up barely attracted much interest at first, but in recent months has exploded into a new and immensely popular social networking site. The niche of Pinterest is its image-based 'pinboard' style of presenting what people share, making it easy to select and share your own interests outside the text-based system that sites like Facebook and Twitter use. This has made it one of the most popular sites in the creative world, as users can easily share and document their artwork, hobbies and interests. This may be why the site is especially popular among women – most of the users are female by quite a wide margin.

From small beginnings and a committed developer, Pinterest was first run as an open-beta site in March 2010 (before that it was in the developmental stages) where members could only join if they received a special invitation from the company. Impressively, Silbermann contacted the first 5,000 users personally, and made sure to give them his personal mobile number in case they needed him for anything whilst using the site or wanted to suggest improvements. Silberman tried to sell his website on around this time, before the website had developed its current impressive user base, but was turned down by the potential buyers as they didn't see much opportunity in an image-based social platform. Presumably, they're none too pleased now.

2011 was the beginning of a new era for the small start up, and the website began to grow exponentially. Still an invitation-based site, the company launched various mobile apps, which were well received by the public, and found themselves in *Time* magazine's *50 Best Websites of 2011* article. By the end of the year, the site had become one of the top ten social networking sites in the world, with 11 million visits each week, and had attracted enormous investment interest; Pinterest had attracted enough attention now to keep growing and growing.

And that's exactly what it did – in 2012 the site revamped its look, changed its terms of service to make it more attractive to independent and business-based users (previously it had retained the right to sell its users' content) and by March had become the third most popular social networking site in the US, after Facebook and Twitter. It was valued at $1.5 billion, and attracted a huge investment of $100 million two months later.

Since 2012, the company has moved from strength to strength and has repeated the pattern set by similar companies like Facebook and Google to buy up other technology start-ups and move them under their own wing. Most notably among these is Pinterest's acquisition of Hackermeter, a developer-based employment site. By October 2013 the company was valued at $3.8 billion, and has more users than ever before. Pinterest is yet another story of the technology start-up gone viral; it's the latest embodiment of the American Dream.

Setting Up Your Pinterest Account

1: Go To https://www.pinterest.com/

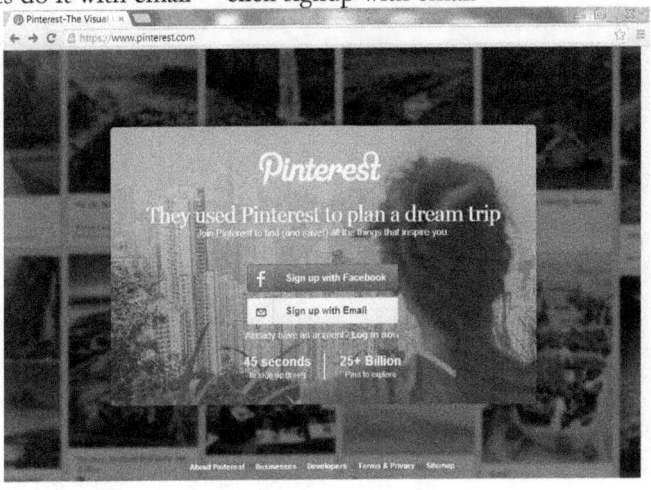

2: Alternatively, you can signup through Facebook too. Lets do it with email - "click signup with email"

You will see this screen upon clicking "signup with email"

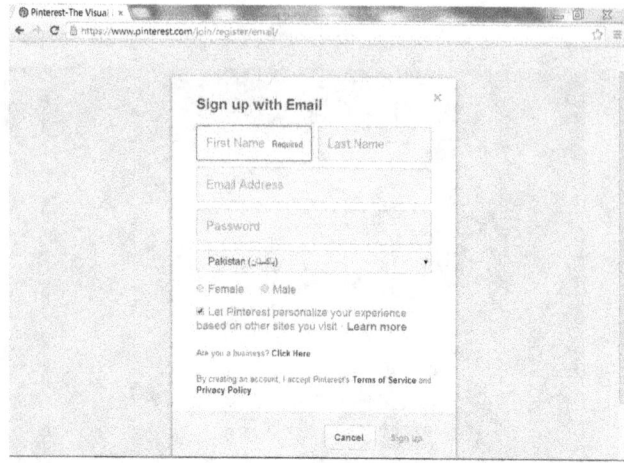

Now fill this form:

1 Full name

2 email

3 Password (easy to remember but hard to guess)

   4 Your location, it will automatically detect (if not you can manually set it).

5 Gender

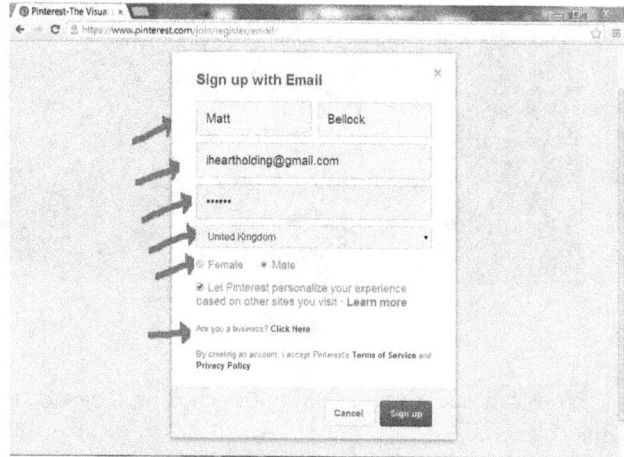

Now click "Sign Up"

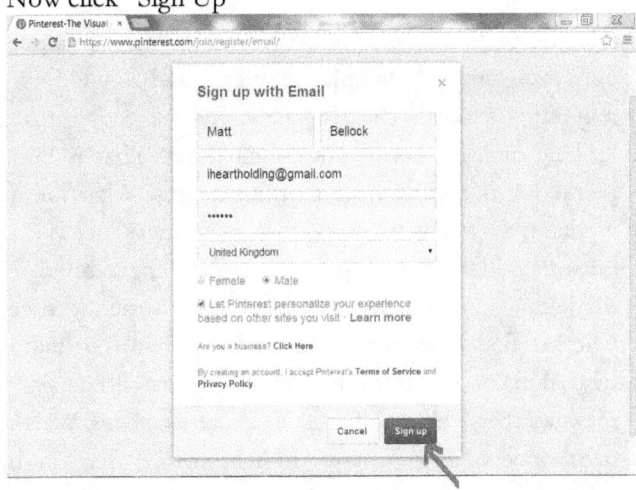

Your profile is all set to go. For a quick tour hit "Next"

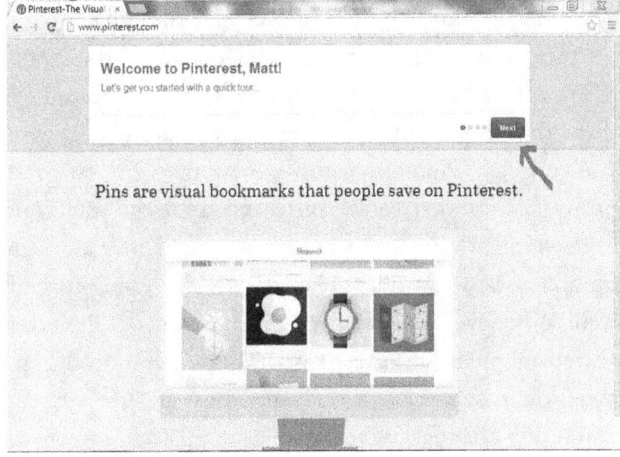

Incorporating Pinterest into Marketing Strategy

One thing that is searched for more than anything by entrepreneurs are templates, plans and blueprints for marketing success. Unfortunately, for the people that are looking at least, there is no such thing. That is because marketing is a very personal thing despite what the mass media may tell you. Marketing a business needs to be personalised to that business. So searching around for a marketing blueprint or a template for marketing success, whether that's through social media channels, or radio, or television, or PR, is wasted time and wasted energy. You may wonder why this fits in to Pinterest then? Well, as I mentioned before Pinterest isn't a channel that sits by it self, it needs to sit alongside other marketing channels to work effectively. That's because if you've hooked the customer in through your Pinterest marketing, they land on your website and nothing looks the same, the messages aren't the same, and the promotions can't be found easily, then they'll probably hit the back button. Likewise, if you've got a Pinterest campaign running for an in store promotion and people turn up and the staff don't understand what they're talking about; there's no signage up and the offer isn't publicised, it's not going to end up well. Whenever you send out a message on Pinterest or any social media channel for that matter, you need to make sure you're sending out the same messages on your other marketing channels, whether that be in store, in your shop windows, on your website, print media, radio, television, or even what your asking your sales representatives to talk about when they go out for meetings. Making sure every ones singing from the same song sheet will help create a much stronger message that the customer sees again and again and understands. Have you ever wondered why television adverts are played so often? How many times have we all seen the Coca Cola advert at Christmas? My guess would be, however old you are, you've seen the advert ten times that age and that's probably a conservative estimate. Why do Coca Cola continue to pay so much money for it to be shown in such prime TV slots? Well, in that instance it is partly for the feel good factor the consumer gets when they see it, but it's also because as consumers it takes a few times of seeing something for the message to really sink in and for us to remember. So, when we put the marketing hat on, what we need to do is, we need to make sure that message is being seen as many times as we can without really annoying the customer. If you're lucky enough to have some television advertising available to you, you need to make sure that the messages that you're sending out, the offers that you're promoting are in line with the ones that you're promoting on the radio, and in print, and on buses, and on social media including Pinterest. Whilst I said at the beginning of this section that there is no tool, blueprint, plan or template that will do this for you, I do have an out line that I like to use. Using Excel across the top row, row A, I like to put the months – January, February, March etc. And then down column A, the first column, I like to put the marketing channels available to me. So, if I'm working for one of my larger clients that might look like- television, radio, newspapers, magazines, social media, website, blog. If I'm working for a smaller, independent retailer, that column might read more like- in store, website, print, local magazines, local radio, social media.

What you've now got is a grid that you can easily see how you're going to translate one promotion across all the campaigns. So at the very top next to January either just before or after, just above or below, you can write in your promotion for January. Perhaps you want to push sign-ups in the gym and the main message is going to be a 'new you'- very original I know. Or maybe, you're a fashion retailer and your main message in January is your January sale. Pop this up at the top where it's nice and easy to see, then do the same for February, March, April, as many months in advance as you'd like to work. Then you need to work down the column. If you're running a January sale, what's your television advert going to look like? What's your radio jingle going to sound like? But, most importantly, what's your Pinterest strategy going to look like in that month? Have a real focus around each month. Months work nicely; people get paid monthly, it's a consumer friendly schedule to work on and it's easy to break down. This is how your Pinterest marketing strategy should sit inside your over arching marketing strategy. And make sure that all the graphics you're using on Pinterest, all the photos that you're using from in-house photography. There all in line with your other channels that' you're using. I work with one company that changes the colour of their logo depending on the season. Make sure that if this is what you do, that you've changed it on your Pinterest account as well. There's nothing worse than a marketing message, whether it be the colour of your logo, the offer, or offer code being used, differ from channel to channel. If I see a red logo on the TV and then I stumble across your Pinterest page and you're using a blue logo, I'm going to wonder whether I've found the right page or not. Keeping your Pinterest marketing channel in line with your other channels will make sure that the efforts that you put into Pinterest marketing will have tangible results and real benefits to your business.

How To Get More Pinterest Followers

There are not many better social platforms to get onto than Pinterest if you're hoping to make some money through social media or to promote something that will. A lot of research has been conducted into Pinterest and a few other sites recently, and results show that this clever little pin-board start up isn't nodding off anytime soon.

Here are some statistics to convince you: first up, there are 70,000,000 Pinterest users. Not bad. In addition to this, 81% of US shoppers have said they trust information on Pinterest, 20% of all online social referrals come from Pinterest *and* it has the highest average order cost of any well-known social network, at $169 per order to Facebook's $95 and Twitter's $70. One single 'pin' on the website generates $0.78 on ecommerce websites and is 'repinned' an average of 10 times! All in all, Pinterest is a good website to establish a hold on, and the more followers you have, the better it'll be for you. That's where we come in; here's our guide to getting as many genuine followers as possible as quickly as possible. You're welcome.

First Things First

The absolute essential first step to getting involved with

Pinterest is to perfect – *perfect* – your profile. This really has to look good, feel good, and be filled with interesting and exciting pins. There's no way you'll attract the followers you want if you look too commercial or too boring or too forced. Try to enjoy making your profile, and make sure it looks genuine; clunky business profiles don't do anywhere near as well as the more relaxed approach. Fill in your about section, include a link to your website, and upload a photo – preferably a headshot; nobody's interested in a logo. After that, things get Pinteresting.

Share As Much As Possible

This logic works for all social networking sites, but Pinterest in particular really needs this approach: be as prolific as possible. That *does not* mean share everything, but try to share as much as possible, follow as many people as possible, repin as many designs as possible, and generally maintain a consistent presence among your followers. Try to connect with your followers, too: ask questions, get them to ask you questions, and have fun with it! The best way to get followers, always, is to enjoy what you're doing.

And what should you share? Well, there's no real right or wrong answer to this. Bare in mind you don't have to just share things that are immediately relevant to your business. Nor do you need to share everything you can find that is relevant. However, it's best to not go completely off the wagon and pin everything you like the look of – try to keep it relevant for the best part. Whatever you decide, make sure that the images are high quality, colourful, and look good! It's an image-based platform, so quality should always come first. For the record, the comforting red, orange and brown hued images are repined about twice as much as blue images.

When you pin any image, Pinterest will always give you the option to follow another board with the same image. Do so, and then repin some more of their images. The next time they log on, you will have cropped up on their (and their followers') radar. Using this technique is a surefire way to get the followers flowing in.

Be Carefully Active

It's been mentioned before, but it's always great to be prolific. But it's not so great if you're unoriginal or uninsightful with it – try to avoid comments like 'nice post' or 'great!' and other variants; they're not in the least bit helpful and won't attract even a little interest. Be witty if you can, caring when you can't, and both when the opportunity presents itself. When you're commenting, head to the most popular pins page and leave some comments there: they're another place where every other user will be and so it's a great place to get some attention. Make sure not the comment on the same post more than three times a day though – the server will automatically assume you're a spam account.

Use popular pin boards and try to interact with people by tagging them (in a positive way) in comments and discussions; and make sure to follow other users as much as you can. Wait to see if they follow you back, though – a high following/followers ratio screams advertising to users, and they'll avoid you. Remember, though, in the US the average Pinterest user follows 9 commercial accounts.

Not bad, but you can bet they're not doing it for the company's sake – it'll be because the company's Pinterest is engaging.

Promote However You Can

There's loads of ways to promote your Pinterest. One of the most simple, of course, is paying for it. If you go down this route, make sure to only promote your most popular boards, as opposed to your entire account. To promote further, make sure to connect your Pinterest account to your Facebook, Twitter, and to whatever else you can. Of course, promotion online is possible as well, and is considerably underrated as a way to bring in web traffic, especially if you're living in a city. Buy some stickers, spend a day out going wild (and photograph it to show your followers) and watch how the extra traffic rolls in.

Holding competitions is another useful way to peak interest in your page. Of course, make sure that the prize is relative to the amount you want your users to do – if they have to repin 20 posts and invite 10 followers to follow you then you better give them a damn good reason to. Make sure to promote it properly, too – use words like 'giveaway' and 'free', and supply an end date. How you select a winner is of course up to you.

The Last Pin

You can look at some statistics for your page by going to pinterest.com/source/yourdomain.com. From here you'll be able to see who is repining your content. Make sure to thank them from time to time; being nice is always better than being business-like when it comes to this kind of thing. Good luck, and happy pinning!

Carry On Pinning

Finally, I guess the only thing to say is to carry on with Pinterest and give it a real go. You've just read the Pinterest setion and you've invested a reasonable amount of time in doing so. You now need to invest time into making Pinterest work for you. No success in any marketing channel, comes over night. You do hear the occasional story where somebody posts a Youtube video and three minutes later it's got five million views. However, these stories are so few and far between that it's very tempting to just call them stories, i.e. they are fictional. For all intents and purposes the amount of videos that get uploaded to Youtube every day, the amount of Pinterest accounts that are created every day, the amount of businesses that decide we're going to use Facebook today means that when one goes viral over night it's the exception that proves the rule that no success is immediate. With Pinterest you really need to give it some time and effort before you can start to see some real success. I'm not saying blindly pin for three years, I'm saying set up your strategy, set up some schedules and timelines and review it once they're over. Give it a good three month or six month trial. Invest that time into it. If you don't seem to be getting any tangible results after one month, don't give up. Dedicate that time and make sure that you don't stop before then. If after three months or six months, whatever your timescale is, you still haven't seen the results you're hoping for then that's the time to review and discuss with yourself or your business partner whether it's right to carry on. It might be that you feel it's just beginning to gain some traction and whilst the results have been poor, you think giving it another two months could produce some real benefit. It might be that you've learnt a lot on the way and another three months would produce the results you've been wanting to see. Inevitably our human nature likes to hope that we will achieve more than we possibly will. It's a bit of a negative note to end the book on, however I hope you understand where I'm coming from. Us entrepreneurs always find the silver lining and we're always over optimistic. Whilst this can be our biggest downfall, if you can turn this round, especially in what some may call defeat, you'll be sure to achieve great things. Not just when it comes to Pinterest, but with all your marketing efforts. Good luck and happy pinning.

6 VINE

Vine is a new application for creating and sharing short video clips. It is available on the iPhone and iPod Touch devices, and the company is working on bringing the app to other platforms. A unique aspect of Vine videos is looping, so the clips automatically play on repeat. In this sense, Vine-created videos resemble animated GIFs.

Vine videos are specially made for sharing short clips. All clips are under six seconds long, which is ideal for sharing memorable moments. The videos are muted by default (but the sound can easily be turned on), they play automatically and they loop endlessly.

Vine was acquired by Twitter in 2012. In this sense, Vine is closely linked to Twitter, though it's possible to use the service even without Twitter. Vine comes with the ability to easily share your videos on Twitter (and Facebook). Also, Twitter has the ability to auto-play Vine videos directly on the site.

So that is what Vine is, but how do we go about using it? Well, Vine makes the process of creating, uploading and sharing videos easy, so anybody can make short clips quickly and easily. It's important to note that Vine uses a special recording technique. The application requires you to touch the screen to record. This way, you can make a continuous six seconds of footage, or you can be creative and make pseudo stop-motion videos. All you need to do is touch the screen to record a frame or series of frames, touch again to stop it, change your scene and record again.

Uploading and sharing is easy. Once a video is created, all you need to do is to click the 'share post' button on the menu. After this, you should choose 'embed' to get the code link you can share on various platforms, such as Twitter. The embeds come in several different sizes (320px, 480px and 600px) and there are also expanded Twitter and Facebook sharing options. You will also be able to see other people's videos, but only if they've decided to share their posts outside of Vine.

Vine appears in a moment of the animated GIF revival. A few years ago, it seemed like GIF as a format was almost outdated. However, fast Internet, better software and certain social media sites have resulted in a sudden rebirth of the animated GIF. It is mainly due to the increasing popularity of short movie clips made into the animated GIF format. Many social media sites, such as Tumblr, are full of these animated GIFs, usually depicting short, 2-5 second long clips from films, TV shows, music videos, etc., neatly edited and converted into the animated GIF format. As a rule, animated GIFs depict interesting and memorable moments and they play on repeat. Vine tries to replicate animated GIFs through short looping videos. The goal is to give users a quick and easy way to make small, memorable videos.

Vine's popularity is on the rise, so its potential as a marketing tool should not be overlooked. Vine offers an app that can potentially reach all demographics. A great thing about Vine is that its clips are a cross between images and videos, which makes an exciting new format companies and professionals can use to present their products and services.

You would have thought six seconds wouldn't be enough to make a narrative video or to present your product in detail, but if you get creative, you will be surprised with what you can achieve. We'll look at one particular case study in just a moment, but for the less creative of you, Vine can easily be used for short but effective product showcases. A quick look at the new handbag you're selling, a tour of a bathroom suite you've just completed, the list goes on. Also, these short videos are ideal for piquing your audience's interest. You can use them to announce a new, exciting offer or to include a short message about your new product that will make people intrigued enough to check out your offer in more detail.

Whilst six seconds probably doesn't strike you as enough time to market your service or product to a gaggle of waiting followers, not too long ago, you would have probably thought the same of 140 characters. Of course, I am making reference to Vine's older sibling here, Twitter. Twitter is a completely different kettle of fish to Vine, but it's living proof that short messages really can work in the world of marketing.

For me though, Vine has the potential to give businesses and marketers so much more than Twitter itself. Despite my previous ramblings about the restricted nature of the traditional tweet, 140 characters is more than enough for a quick message, combined with a link to a much longer article or sales pitch or marketing landing page or wherever else you decide to send your Twitter followers. Vine really is a restrictive platform though. Six seconds is *all* you get. Nothing more. Whilst many will see this as a restriction, I think the best marketers and business owners will see this as a license to get creative. Yes, you could place a link at the end of the video, but in reality, I doubt many people would then spend the time typing that link into their browser, just to be bombarded with your sales pitch. Instead, Vine can be the ideal platform for a bit of creativity.

Taking a look at some brands that have already taken to Vine can provide some clues as to what will work, but rather than hunting around for the most creative ways to use Vine, I've done the hard work for you and found, in my opinion, an example of a truly great Vine. I'm talking about Glynis, over at SweetShot Photography, who got creative with a Vine. The Boston based photographer showed off her equipment, before offering the empty stool to the viewer. Whilst it doesn't sound ground-breaking, it certainly works better than a traditional 'Tweet with picture/link' combination. Can you imagine the interest in a simple, *"We take really cool headshots like in this picture: <PICTURE> Find out more here: <LINK>"*. None. By using a few short clips, Glynis markets her service by telling a story. Firstly, she shows off her equipment. The right equipment is important to a photographer, and most people who go to have their photo taken professionally will be hoping that the photographer has all the proper gear. By picturing it, she's showing she does. In fact, in this particular instance, it perhaps works better than a traditional 'equipment' page found on so many other photographers' websites. For the viewer, we think, 'big Nikon DSLR camera, she's got the proper stuff'. That's all it takes. We're not bored with the details, the shutter speed, and the lens ratio times by aperture size.[9] After a quick rush round some other bits and bobs, we're shown her business card. Read: 'Branding? Check.' Again, no faffing around with fancy company formation stories, it's just a simple second-long video clip of a business card. But that is all it took. We then move on to the empty chair before panning out and seeing the whole setup. Accompanying the video is the simple line, *'Studio is ready and waiting for you! HEADSHOTS!!!'*. By showing the empty chair, we are, as an audience, being invited in. We're being told this seat is empty, but you'd look great on it. This simple Vine is one of the best pieces of marketing I have seen in a long while. It's simple, tells a story, and places the customer in the story, making the sale effortless. Glynis is inviting us to sit in the chair and relax, because she will take care of the rest. Needless to say, the Vine was a success, and from what I've heard Glynis was impressed with the 'return on investment'.

---

[9] Ok, I made that last one up. I think.

7 A FEW FINAL WORDS AND A FREE LUNCH

There are millions of websites on the Internet, many of them claiming to have the best advice for those looking for Facebook business tips and tricks. We all know however, that these websites are not all as legitimate as others. The following list offers itself as an initial guide for further research and advice, but please do bear in mind what I mentioned in my TED talk. If you find a resource that is talking about your customers as if they were a piece of meat, please close the browser window and send me an email instead. I'd rather help each and every one of you individually, than to let you go implementing terrible advice from somebody who couldn't care less about you, or your customers. Anyway, here's my list of places that are (fairly) reliable in alphabetical order.

- Amy Porterfield
- Bloggers Make Money
- Boom Social

- Brands With Fans
- Christian Karasiewicz
- Danny Brown
- Dustn.tv
- Jenn's Trends
- Jon Loomer
- Likeable Daily
- Moz
- Muddywall
- Pagemodo
- Post Planner
- Pushing Social
- RazorSocial
- Simply Measured
- Social Media Frontiers
- Socially Sorted
- Socially Stacked
- SocialMouths
- Spiderworking
- Top Dog Social Media

If you think I've missed something out, or you wanted to know a bit more about any one of the examples I've given, please get in touch and I'll be more than happy to expand upon points, along with make a note to include it in further revisions. You can email me at:

info@lewislove.co.uk

This book was a long time in the making. I wanted to steer clear of the typical marketing books that treat customers as meat, instead focusing on the broader picture. I've spent a lot of sleepless nights, drafting up notes, going through chapters with my editor and I'd really appreciate it if you could spare a moment to review my book on Amazon.

I'd love to hear your opinions on the book! It would be great to hear your story, and be able to offer you specific, personal guidance. You've just read my book, the least I could do is offer you some friendly advice! After all, it's all about being sociable, isn't it?

Thank you for reading my book. I hope you've enjoyed it as much as I enjoyed writing it.

ABOUT THE AUTHOR

Lewis Love is a new media consultant based in Derbyshire, UK. Originally from Essex, Lewis worked on the breakfast show of a radio station for 18 months before travelling around the world. Upon his return, he moved to the midlands to study Media Studies at the University of Derby. He was the student representative for his course for three years, and in 2012, he was awarded the University of Derby Award Student of the Year for his work with local businesses. Since then, he's worked with start-ups in the fashion industry to multi-national, multi-million corporations, advising, educating and occasionally amusing them on how best to implement digital marketing strategies and enhance their online presence.

Besides his work online, Lewis enjoys spending time with his girlfriend, Emily, whom he lives with in Derby. He's an Arsenal fan, although he kindly asks you not to hold that against him, and he enjoys a craft beer from time to time; produced by smaller, passionate breweries of course.

* 9 7 8 1 4 9 9 5 5 5 3 7 0 *